The University of Texas
Division of Extension
Extension Teaching Centers
Extension Bldg. 302
Austin 12

Recd 6/18/52

JEALOUSY IN CHILDREN

A GUIDE FOR PARENTS

Jealousy in Children

A GUIDE FOR PARENTS

BY EDMUND ZIMAN, M.D.

Former Senior Medical Officer (Psychiatrist),
St. Elizabeths Hospital, Washington, D. C.

New York : A. A. WYN, INC. : 1949

DESIGNED BY GEORGE HORNBY

PRINTED IN THE UNITED STATES OF AMERICA
AMERICAN BOOK–STRATFORD PRESS, INC., NEW YORK

TO MY WIFE

Introduction

IF I WERE asked to name the one problem in family relationships most frequently troublesome to parents, I would select jealousy. It is a basic human emotion. It creates difficulties in living because it's unpleasant; we don't like to feel it, we don't like to see it in ourselves, and we don't like to see it in our children. In our work in our Child Guidance Clinic we find problems manifesting jealous emotions in practically every case, whether there is only one child or several children in the family. We are frequently requested to give talks on the subject to groups of parents and receive numerous questions from parents who are eager to discover ways of eliminating disturbing jealous behavior they observe in their children. Sometimes it is difficult to interpret behavior that is expressive of jealousy to parents who do not want to believe that it could possibly happen in their family. One of the problems we have to deal with, as Mental Hygiene educators as well as therapists, is how to help people to learn to accept jealousy as a reality and how to help them develop constructive techniques of dealing with jealousy in themselves and in their children.

When we are faced with an unpleasant situation we make efforts to deny it, avoid it, suppress it, or get rid of it. It doesn't seem to matter that these operations rarely if ever succeed. If we deny it the facts are there to taunt us; if we avoid it we eliminate parts of our experience that can be useful to us; if we suppress it we have to maintain a kind of armed militia to keep guard against the escape of the dangerous information or feeling, which will inevitably escape in some disguised form anyway. In other words, anything we do other than facing the facts and learning to accept them uses up our energy resources, interferes with satisfactory living, and gives us more anxiety than we would have in facing the reality. Such is the case in dealing with jealousy too. We may try to hide it but it is still there to bother us. If we have anxieties about our own jealous feelings, we will communicate them to our children and the problem will be made worse. If we can learn to accept jealousy in ourselves and others, to respect our right and the rights of others to feel jealous on occasion, we won't feel so concerned about it. Then we will be able to respect it, to sympathize when it is appropriate, to help our children when it seems to be troublesome for them.

An important part of the contribution Dr. Ziman makes in this book is to bring the problem into the open, so that all of us may look at it. In clear, nontechnical language he describes the signs and causes of jealousy, when and how it occurs, and what we may do about it. The book is designed for parents, but should prove to be of considerable interest as well to educators, counselors, and all who are concerned with popular education about mental health.

WILLIAM L. GRANATIR, M.D.
Director, Washington Institute of Mental Hygiene
Washington, D.C.

Preface

WHAT makes a three-year-old child suddenly begin bed wetting, after he has been so well trained? And when an eight-year-old girl asks for a nursing bottle, should she be allowed to have one? Why should these things happen just after a new baby arrives? This book tells why the three-year-old reverts to bed wetting and the eight-year-old asks for a bottle; it tries to show how to handle these problems.

Knowing *what* to do may be all that is needed, in some instances. But I feel very strongly that it's more important to understand *why* the difficulties began in the first place. The first part of the book tries to explain the ways of children; the rest of the book shows how to handle the problem of jealousy as it occurs in different situations.

I was helped a lot with this book by many people. To all of them, my heartfelt thanks. Cosette Saslaw was very patient with me and gave in to my very unreasonable demands on her time; at the Washington Institute of Mental Hygiene, Thelma Du Vinage, Isabelle Phillips, and Mary Schwarz, of the staff, gave me valuable help; Florence Weller Peter and Madeleine A. Deutsch, of the Work and Play School in New York City, made helpful suggestions; Mary H. Frank read the entire manuscript, and gave me many invaluable suggestions as to the inclusion of material to round out the presentation.

It goes without saying that no part of this book would have been written were it not for my association with

St. Elizabeths Hospital in Washington, the Washington-Baltimore Psychoanalytic Institute, and the William Alanson White Institute of Psychiatry. To my teachers there go my warmest thanks.

EDMUND ZIMAN, M.D.
New York City

Contents

JEALOUSY IN CHILDREN

A GUIDE FOR PARENTS

CHAPTER I

Signs of Jealousy in Children

PARENTS are becoming more and more aware that jealousy in children is often a very real problem. And not knowing what to do about it, many parents are worried. Perhaps they have one baby and are thinking of having another, or they have two children and may have noticed signs of jealousy in one or the other. Their questions may run like this: "Do you think spacing them further apart is better?" "I've read somewhere that you should have your children close together . . ." "My children aren't jealous of each other—I think . . . Of course, the younger one was a problem but I believe we handled it well . . ." "I've heard you may run into the problem of jealousy if . . ."

"You *will* run into jealousy," I want to tell them. "Whether you have two children or ten children, there will be jealousy; and if you have only one child, you will still run into jealousy."

There will be jealousy, but the depth of jealous feeling will vary with each child. It will depend on his relationship to his parents, his preparation for the coming of a new baby, and his parents' attitudes toward him in general: whether they enjoy him and love him, or whether their affection depends on his good behavior. It will depend, too, on whether both parents understand the child's upsets and whether both agree on the approach to his problems. In a large family it will depend on the parents' understanding of each child, so that no child is overlooked or slighted, or compared unfavorably with the others. But while jealousy in children is almost completely unavoidable, it need not become a problem. Knowing this, most parents will try to do something about it; and jealousy, like the other difficulties in living which bother us from time to time, can be less serious if it is dealt with properly.

I hope that this book will give perspective on such problems and show how parents may solve them very simply and successfully. But the problem can be very serious. For there is danger where jealousy is permitted to exist without being recognized. I know that statements like this are abhorred by many parents. "Please leave us alone," they say, "what was good enough for our grandparents is good enough for our children." Such parents refuse to believe that anything but harm can come of what they call alarmist propaganda, despite the evidence. It is an encouraging sign that such parents are in a minority today and that a greater number of parents are becoming aware that the answer is not so very simple. Today educators, psychologists, psychoanalysts, and pediatricians agree that where emotional problems are recognized early enough, and something is done about them, there will be fewer emotional difficulties later in life.

Perhaps we are more familiar with jealousy as seen in adults than with any other strong emotion except love. Jealousy is the basis for a large number of current novels, plays, movies, and radio sketches; newspapers headline cruelty, murder, and suicide, involving extremely jealous individuals. It is not surprising, then, that a discussion of jealousy in children should provoke some unrest in parents. The word has become associated with an extremely unpleasant and destructive emotional disturbance which we do not like to admit may be present in our children.

At this point I ought to emphasize that jealousy, the green-eyed monster which bothers adults, is not quite the same as a child's jealousy. In the first place, jealousy in the adult may be rooted in many different sorts of childhood disturbances and is not necessarily a carry-over of earlier jealousy. Furthermore, jealousy in a child is a perfectly normal reaction; usu-

ally it is an unconscious attitude or feeling which bothers
him and makes him as uncomfortable as it does his parents.
It is the poor handling, the mismanagement, of jealousy
which causes trouble, not the feeling itself; it is the failure of
the parents to recognize the existence of jealousy, or their
downright suppression of it, that produces such unhappy results.

Finally, a jealous child does not necessarily grow up to be a
jealous adult. He may show other symptoms of his childhood
disturbance later on; he may become ambitious, striving,
or overaggressive in order to gain the prestige and security he
didn't find as a child. He may have other outlets and activities which are the result of his earlier jealousy without actually being jealous.

Jealousy may make a child misbehave: his misbehavior is
the *symptom* of a worry. When a child is ill, the symptoms of
his illness may be a cough, a running nose, fever, an upset
stomach, and so on. His mother would hesitate to give him
pills unless she knew what the specific illness was. It is just
as futile to try to get rid of the signs of jealousy, the misbehavior, without understanding the source.

Part of the function of this book is to show how jealousy
manifests itself in children, so that parents will be able to
recognize the condition when they run across it. I should explain, at this point, that I intend to consider jealousy and
envy as one and the same thing. There are many more or
less technical differences between them, most of which I have
no real argument with, but it will be much easier to think
of jealousy as envy too. Thus we can say that *a child is jealous when he wants something someone else has.* We can look
on this as the basic definition. "Someone else" may be a
brother or a sister, or his father or mother, or anyone else.
"Wants" implies that he may feel deprived of what was once
his, and would like to have it again. "Has" need not mean
actual possession of the "something"; a child need only imagine that someone else has it.

The word "something" is important, and for a young child

it means basically love, understanding, and protection. A child may feel that his mother is giving these things to someone else, not to him; love, understanding, and protection, in his mind, are represented by Popsicles, new shoes, praise from Aunt Dorothy, the difference between a red balloon and a yellow one, an extra spoonful of ice cream, or a good report card.

The child who is troubled has to find some way of showing it. Therefore, when he is bothered by the loss of his parents' love—when he thinks their love has now been transferred to his brother or sister—he is jealous. His emotional problem is there and we have the evidence that it exists because he develops, and shows, the symptoms of jealousy.

For example, a two-year-old who has been successfully toilet-trained may forget what he has been taught when the new baby arrives; he may revert to his infantile habits of no toilet training. When he does, he shouldn't be punished or shamed; most two-year-olds are not completely toilet-trained; his parents should just say he is reverting to his infantile habits, and ask "Why?" He may strike his infant sister, or pull her out of her crib, or worse, but he shouldn't be regarded with horror, as if his mother and father had suddenly found out that they were the parents of a small monster. They should ask themselves "Why?" The chances are the child himself is too young to know the answer.

If the parents consider his behavior depraved, malicious, selfish, or feel that he is backward, they will be tempted to punish him or ignore him, as the case may be. The danger is in this: while they may achieve temporary results, they are ignoring the condition—the illness—which brought on these symptoms.

In the same way, if they fail to see that their child's maliciousness or selfishness are symptoms, they are apt to overlook the underlying cause. There's a difference between saying: "He's a malicious child" and "He's *acting* in a malicious manner." The first statement is a diagnosis of an illness; you are calling it malice, and the treatment for malice is limited:

you punish him and hope that he will be less malicious, or kinder, or whatever. But when you recognize malice for what it is, a symptom, you are correct in saying that he is acting in a malicious manner. A child acts malicious not because he is basically malicious, but because he is emotionally disturbed. Sometimes this is how emotional difficulties arise: in an older child, for example, the difficulty may start when the new baby is born. The parents pay more attention to the new baby than they do to the older child, who becomes unsure of their love; he becomes unsure of himself because he doesn't know what he has done to make them love him less; he blames it on the new baby; he is jealous; he is malicious to the baby.

They cannot get very far by punishing him for his malice, because they have not reassured him that he has not lost his parents' love; punishment, on the other hand, will only help convince him that he has. Malice serves a purpose for the child, too: he needs to be malicious to make himself feel more important, and he feels important when he shows he is superior to the new baby. But maliciousness can be harmful when it arouses the disapproval of his parents, and then arouses self-disapproval, so that he thinks less of himself. Therefore, to help the child we have to get at the underlying feeling, and when that is released the misbehavior will go along with it.

There was the mother who told a child psychiatrist that her son was becoming a problem. In the past three months he had been sent home from kindergarten at least once a week because he soiled himself, even though the children were taken to the toilet regularly. He was six; it began the day after his sister's second birthday. After hearing more of the story the doctor told the mother that he thought the little boy was jealous. The mother laughed. "David jealous? Because I gave Holley a doll for her birthday? After all, he's a big boy now."

Another mother complained of her son's refusal to go to school, or to play with other boys. He preferred to stay near

her. "Junior was *so* active and even played with boys bigger
than himself. I can't understand it. And then, to make mat-
ters worse . . ." She was embarrassed. The doctor asked her to
continue. "I haven't told his father; he would never get over
it. Imagine a boy of seven wanting a bottle just because his
baby brother was getting his!"

Children are jealous when they want something someone
else has. David's sister Holley was given a doll; whatever she
was given became a symbol of love, so far as he was concerned. It could have been a blanket, a pair of shoes, or straw-
berry-colored Jello when he had lime. That Holley was given
a doll meant that she was loved more—and he less.

Junior, the seven-year-old, must have watched longingly
for months while his baby brother was given his bottle. He
was jealous, no doubt about it, but he said nothing, because
he knew his parents would not approve if he complained.
They liked the baby even if he didn't; this gave him reason
to believe that *he* was wrong, not they. He would watch
quietly while the baby was given the bottle, and he hoped
his mother would understand and offer him one, too. Eventually, he could no longer hold it in—he *had* to ask, which was
in itself a blow to his pride; he was embarrassed to tears that
his father might find out. Also, here was corroboration of his
feeling that, in her dealings with him, his mother lacked understanding. *Before* the baby was born, he was the center of
everything, and now it was the baby who seemed to attract
all the attention. The bottle signified to him not merely food
but his mother's attention and love and all the things which
go with being fed and held and cuddled.

And there was Jane's mother. "I punished her for striking Alice. Alice is older, and knows better, but Jane pro-
vokes all the fights." Jane, at the age of eight, still sucked her
thumb; not unusual, but it can be a signal of distress.

Jane had long since given up any idea that her mother
would protect her from her older sister, even when Alice
started the fights. Alice had been an invalid for a few years,
and had taken full advantage of the situation. She was never

disciplined, but Jane was, and Jane was jealous. Like David and Junior, she wanted something someone else had; they were all getting less love, little understanding, and a minimum of protection.

Parents often think that children jump to conclusions, that they are precocious when they see even *one* side of an argument. Maturity, we hope, brings with it the ability to reason, to see both sides of a question, and to draw inferences. These three mothers loved their children, I know, and never intended to create jealousy between them by loving one more than the other. They were naturally troubled: "David is too sensitive," his mother said. "He knows I love him. It isn't possible that just because I gave Holley a doll . . . If children could only understand . . ." However, David *is* sensitive and he does jump to conclusions. All he knows is that he was loved for four years; he liked it; during those four years he was unhappy only when he thought his mother loved him less, as when she loved his father. But when the baby came, he began to understand that his early suspicions were true: now she loved the baby. He saw that his parents paid more attention to the baby; it did not enter his head that the baby was small and weak and helpless, that his parents had to pay more attention to her. He had his choice of hundreds of incidents each day; he could point to any or all of them as further examples of how he was pushed aside.

When this was explained to David's mother, she saw that David was thinking logically, all right, but that she had not understood. It took a little time to straighten things out in that family and in the other two, but eventually David no longer soiled himself in school, Junior did not withdraw from his friends, and Jane stopped sucking her thumb. Their parents had not known the children were jealous; they were worried about the symptoms. But once the symptoms were understood, and recognized as signs of jealousy, the problems were immensely simplified.

Few children come right out and say they are jealous. The child who is less than two years old when the new baby is

born may forget what little toilet training he knows, or perhaps he begins to awaken at odd and inconvenient hours. He
has become aware of the presence of an intruder who is taking up even part of the time his parents once devoted to him,
and he demands his rights. He can't express himself in words,
but he feels disturbed and shows it! His groping little hands
which could not co-ordinate before now sweep ashtrays to
the floor with an unerring instinct for complete and noisy
destruction. All of his activities, if you study them, leave
little doubt as to his real feelings for the baby.

I have in mind two-year-old Georgiana and her brother,
Johnny. They are both the same age for two weeks of each
year: John was born less than a year after his sister. Although
Georgiana is very little, she knows what behavior is expected
of her. When she is asked—or told, as far as she is concerned—
to "love" Johnny, she goes to him and gives him a great
big hug. Everybody, including Johnny, beams—except Georgiana. She is only a little less stern than when she carefully removes all of her toys and Johnny's from his playpen and de-
posits them in hers. She doesn't play with them—she merely
wants to make certain that *he* doesn't have them. She is not
as interested in her own things as she is in his; her broken
toys are immediately replaced by duplicates from Johnny's
collection, since both are always given identical gifts. In contrast to this great awareness of his presence, her disregard of
him is sometimes shocking—and dangerous—as when she
charges around the house at great speed, while he tries to
follow. Her race track is the first floor of the house; it includes the living room, dining room, and entrance hall. When
she overtakes him, he gets hurt, because she knocks him
down; her attitude is a mixture of impatience and disdain, as
if he is much too small and incompetent to be regarded as
anything but one of the milder annoyances one has to put
up with.

Of course, we rarely find two children born so close together in one family (except twins), but it is a dramatic ex-

ample of jealousy in a child too young to express herself clearly. She is showing her resentment of his intrusion into the world she controlled for almost a year. The fact is she must have been aware that some change had taken place, that somebody else was getting the attention that was rightfully hers. A little child needs to feel loved and needs to have this love demonstrated even more when there is a new baby. The reassurance that she belongs, that she is still very lovable, that she was and is a nice child, needs repetition over and over in both words and acts. Parents are best equipped to give this intimate, constant reassurance, but they need to be reminded of its importance. Even the most devoted parents become preoccupied with a new infant, and are sometimes not aware of the older child's need, though their basic feelings of love and devotion to the child have not altered or diminished. Georgiana, when she showed jealousy, probably seemed most unlovable to her parents and other onlookers. Really, at those very moments she was most in need of sympathy and patience.

Sometimes a two-year-old girl who cannot express her feelings and shows few outward signs of jealousy toward the baby will show her feelings in doll play, or in playing with other children.

One teacher in a nursery school noted that a very well-behaved, carefully toilet-trained youngster repeated this behavior pattern over and over: she would pick up a doll, cuddle it, talk lovingly to it, and suddenly throw it on the floor. Then she would pick it up again, and say: "Poor baby, poor darling," and once more throw it with all her strength. Another nursery school record tells of a very friendly, seemingly happy two-year-old boy, with a younger brother, who would play easily and freely with the other two-year-olds until suddenly and without warning he would bite the child nearest him.

In both of these cases the teacher was able, through conferences with the mother, to point out that these were

The University of Texas
Division of Extension
Extension Teaching Centers
Extension Bldg. 302
Austin 12

signs of the child's disturbance—of jealousy. And the parents, in turn, were able to give the children added reassurance and attention.

Very young children will rarely show the more obvious signs of jealousy; their jealousy is usually disguised in some way. When they fail to impress their parents with their displeasure at the new baby, their hatred for the baby increases, but is repressed—hidden from the eyes of the world, eventually from themselves. Too many times such repression is the direct result of fearing their parents' disapproval. Georgiana represses her feelings toward Johnny because her parents tell her she is malicious when she takes his toys away from him and she is vicious when she knocks him down, but she is such a good child when she follows their orders to love him. Her parents are successfully making her repress her true feelings now, but those feelings may come back, in some more harmful form, later on.

At this point it would be well for parents to recognize that a child may be ambivalent in his feelings, not only toward a brother or sister, but toward his parents as well. Ambivalent means feelings of love and hate toward the same person; he may want to love the baby, he may really enjoy it at times, but at the same time he hates it for having usurped his place. An older child is more articulate and will even tell you as much at times. It is not wrong or wicked for the child to feel this way—it is part of an awareness of other human beings and of one's own feelings. It becomes dangerous only when it is called wrong or bad or if the feeling is not allowed expression.

One young woman I have heard about, thirty-six and unmarried, is eighteen months older than her sister. During the course of her psychoanalysis something came up which seemed to point out the existence of jealousy when she was an infant: her first memory is of the day her sister was born. When she was about seven, she told her mother that she remembered a room painted pale blue, her mother in a brass bed in the corner, an old woman and a man with a beard near the bed.

There was a baby crying, and she was crying, too. She remembered that she was in a crib in the same room, standing up. Her mother and father were amazed, and corroborated the facts: she was asleep in her crib in her parents' pale blue bedroom at the time her sister was born; the bearded man was the family doctor; the old woman was the midwife. Her mother remembered that she had awakened and cried when the newborn baby cried, and her father had to come in to soothe her—and change her, too. Also, the family had moved from that house about a month later, and never had a pale blue bedroom again, or a brass bed.

Many people can remember as their first memory the day of the birth of the next child, or some incident in relation to a new baby. It is most impressive when this is something that happened before the age of three. I am quite willing to agree that the "memory" may actually be an unconscious reconstruction of statements overheard much later and mistaken for a memory, but the mistake itself is important. Why should such a mistake be made, unless the child is more than mildly impressed with some aspect or other of the baby's arrival? The patient never realized the implications of remembering the incident; there was evidence, before she recalled this memory, that she was jealous of her sister when they were infants. But somehow this memory was so impressive that soon other "forgotten" details were remembered, and helped her in her treatment.

When the older child is three or more, the birth of the baby will cause resentment which is more easily detected, because the older child can express his feelings verbally. He may show mild interest in the baby, or ignore it, but sooner or later his true feelings will come out. "O.K." he will say, "now let's send her back to the hospital." Or, "You gonna keep her any longer?" Or, "She's too little," or too red, or too noisy. Of course, the only trouble with the baby is that she is making too many demands on his parents and he feels threatened. A friend told me that his son, Peter, who was four when his baby sister was born, dutifully admired her for a week. Then one day he asked his father: "Don't babies ever die?"

As parents grow to be more experienced they come to realize that these seemingly callous remarks are not limited to early childhood, nor confined to jealousy. Children are just not sentimental. Death and loss are too confused, too unreal, to be comprehended fully. I know of an eight-year-old boy who had a long, interesting conversation with his mother about what he would inherit when his parents died. He is not a calculating child, nor grasping, but he just didn't consider that death means separation, too. However, you can be sure that a child must be fairly confident of his parents' approval and love to be able to state his feelings openly and directly.

As we discuss the problem of jealousy and list instances and examples of the way it is shown in children, it becomes fairly evident that spacing the children farther apart, or having them close to one another in age doesn't seem to make very much difference. When children are close together, it may mean that the mother is worn out from constant feeding, diapering, making formulas, so that she is less apt to be patient and understanding with a jealous child. Or the older child, who is still really a baby, may be forced to take more responsibility for himself, his toys, his behavior when he is not ready for it.

Jealousy is not hereditary. Children are not born with temperamental factors which make one child more vulnerable, more apt to be intensely distressed when a new baby arrives. But sometimes the first child (or the second, or the third) is born at a time when parents are unprepared financially or emotionally for a child. Young parents often have a difficult time adjusting to a third and very demanding member of the family. Or, as happened in wartime, the father may be absent, which imposes a good deal of strain on mother and baby. Or the eldest child may have had to bear the brunt of the psychological theories of a few years back, which said you mustn't pick up your baby too often—let him cry it out, if the clock doesn't specify feeding time. Or the mother may have spent more time with one child and less with another because of a job, illness, family upsets, or a divorce. All of these factors will make a child less ready to accept a brother or sister and less able to work out of his doubts as to his place in the family.

But no matter how many courses we have had in child care, we cannot anticipate all of our children's problems. Each child is different; each situation is new. Each child will be a different personality from all others if only because he is in a specific family at a certain stage of its growth and because he is born to parents with reactions and feelings that are peculiar to themselves and to no one else.

There is no stigma attached to having such problems. Actually, when we face each emotional difficulty in ourselves, or in our children, as it is presented to us, there is no problem—it is a part of learning and growing, and it is much wiser to grow by and with our emotions than to leave them in an unsolved, childish state.

The problem of jealousy isn't confined to the home. One has to watch for its signs and symptoms in school, and wherever children work or play together. We talk of the spirit of competition as one of the virtues so needed for our development. Psychiatrists call it competitiveness when it has its beginnings in the family, as between brothers and sisters. This form of competition may be the result of jealousy in the home, where the children are competing for their parents' affection and approval. Such competition in the family, between brothers and sisters, is known as "sibling rivalry"; it can be brought on by any situation where one child suspects that the other children are getting more love, protection, or understanding from their parents. It can take the form of the so-called "bid for attention," which is the result of a *need* for attention and which indicates that the child feels he isn't getting enough attention, or that someone else is getting more. Most of the signs of jealousy are actually the jealous child's attempts to get attention in one way or another. After he has tried, over and over again, to show how much better he is than his brothers and sisters, the habit becomes fixed, and he may go on competing in school, on the playground, and later in the business world.

It is hard to estimate how many experiences of defeat a child can stand before he comes to expect defeat and to be resigned to it. Sometimes he believes he *has* to lose because of some inadequacy on his part which prevents his winning out. On the other hand, sometimes he tries to prove he really is not inadequate, so he continues to compete. When he gets used to it, and expects defeat continually, he may withdraw and become submissive, while another child who has to keep on trying to prove that he is *not* inadequate may become aggressive.

Children compete not only with each other but also with one parent for the affection of the other; this is jealousy, too. This is a part of the Oedipus complex, the love relationship between a child and a parent of the opposite sex. A little boy who is attached to his mother may be openly resentful of his father's attention to her. He may say something like: "Go away, Daddy," or he may push him away. It takes a wise and loving father to understand such rejection. A little girl may resent her mother's presence because she adores her father and wants his love for herself. Again, the mother will have to understand what is happening so that she will not be tempted to compete with her daughter.

According to Freud, the Oedipus complex is based upon a sexual love between a child and the parent of the opposite sex. We should add that Freud meant "sexual" to include all the manifestations of a love relationship and not necessarily the physical aspects of it alone. A child's jealousy, then, can be complicated by the love for one parent and resentment of the other, as well as by the parents' response to the child's feelings.

I hope that this book will help parents to see that their particular situation, or that of their children, or any situation which needs help, can indeed be helped. Let me say again that children are jealous as a matter of course; it is normal and proper and to be expected. It need not become a problem, but when it does, it can be taken care of. A certain amount of competitiveness and rivalry is normal in children and in grownups, and may even be essential, but even if this takes the form of a neurosis it can be taken care of, if not by the parents, then by a child-guidance clinic, or a child psychiatrist, or a psychoanalyst. Reading the next few chapters should make it clear that it is not shameful for parents to take their child to someone for psychiatric help, not any more shameful than getting medical help when a medical problem is beyond their control. We know that too few children are seen by psychiatrists, not because there are less psychiatric problems than medical or surgical ones, but because the psychiatric difficulties are less frequently recognized.

Today we are trying to provide health care and protection for infants and children so that we can guard them from the often serious consequences of childhood diseases; sometimes by simple and inexpensive treatment we can correct conditions that might later become handicaps. In the field of mental hygiene we are learning how to recognize the early indications of emotional disturbances and personality problems, which are the first signs of a child's inability to meet the demands and frustrations of life. And we are increasingly able to provide much needed help to these children so that they won't become permanently handicapped because of their early difficulties. We are discovering more proof all the time that the parents themselves are most important and effective agents in the promotion of good mental health of children. They can do what no one else can do: they can provide the warm understanding, the care, and the guidance which every child needs.

CHAPTER II

Guilt Feelings in Parents

BECAUSE so many parents genuinely want help on the problem of jealousy I feel that it is necessary to point out in this chapter a few of the difficulties which may stand in their way. Most individuals are not wholly objective about their problems, especially their emotional difficulties. Every psychiatrist and every psychoanalyst has to help his patients see what lies behind their present behavior, to find out what it is that really bothers them. That isn't easy and can't be done overnight. People rationalize and hide their true feelings from themselves because it is a blow to their self-esteem to have to admit that they are hostile or insecure, or even that they may make honest mistakes.

This is very understandable. We spend our lives building up our defenses, protecting ourselves psychologically, not admitting that we are worried, afraid, or unhappy; we find it very hard to confess that we are covering up—we don't even want to admit it to ourselves.

As parents we are on the defensive, too. If our children show signs of disturbance we feel it is a reflection on our own ability as parents. It is not easy to admit we have made mistakes, particularly where our children are concerned. There are always neighbors and relatives around to make us feel uncomfortable about their misbehavior.

Most mothers and fathers want to be good parents. Perhaps that is why some of them are unwilling to admit that there is such a thing as jealousy in their families. It would be a sign of failure as parents and therefore a blow to their own self-esteem. This is not unusual. You know people who take offense at the slightest suggestion of criticism, whether it concerns their jobs, their characters, or their efficiency as parents.

One father (whose chief complaint was an uncontrollable temper) told his doctor over and over again during the course of his psychoanalysis: "There is nothing wrong with Freddy. It's the older one, Nora, that we have trouble with. She is a completely unlovable child." He gave examples of Nora's maliciousness, her refusal to help with the housework, her lack of humor. He said she never showed any affection for his wife or for him. Although she was at the top of her class in intermediate school and seemed to be popular with her classmates, she never talked about her activities there, nor about her other experiences away from home. In fact, she rarely talked: "If she can get out of doing the dishes, she escapes to the living room, turns on the radio, and reads. Never get a civil word out of her even when she *does* talk. It's a snarl sometimes, or maybe she'll grunt when someone asks her a question."

Then came word from school that she was not doing as well as before. Her class work was excellent, as always, but her deportment was poor. She had begun to play with a gang made up of the most mischievous children in the neighborhood. These children had more money than the rest, made more noise, played violent games, and were very clannish. Nora did their homework for them and allowed them to copy from her when the class was given written tests. "She seems to have some need to run around with this group of children," her father was told by her teacher. "She allows them to copy her work to stay on good terms with them in their activities after school."

Nora's father had made mistakes as a parent. He hadn't meant to; they were honest mistakes, not at all deliberate. In order to protect his position as a parent he felt that he had to defend himself, and discovered, as do most chronic self-defenders, that the best defense is to become offensive. *He* accused his *daughter* of being unlovable. Why not? She acted as if she were unlovable from the time Freddy was born. But there was this question in the back of his mind: hadn't she been lovable before that? Had she changed because she was jealous of Freddy? Why had he failed to recognize it? He had felt for a long time that perhaps he was to blame, but he could not admit it to himself.

He wasn't, you can be sure, blaming himself for making the same mistakes all parents make, even though he said so. His unkindness was the clue: he felt guilty because he was so hard and unbending in his attitudes toward her; he was offensive, a cruel father, and he felt that was inexcusable. His guilt arose by these steps: first, he blamed himself for Nora's reaction to Freddy's presence; second, he blamed himself for her early signs of jealousy; third, he blamed himself for his harshness to her. Now, Nora's reaction to Freddy, her jealousy of the new baby, was somewhat excusable because he just did not know. He blamed himself more than he should have. His resentment increased because her jealousy showed him up as a bad parent, and when this resentment turned into harshness, he had a *real* reason to be guilty.

But there was something else involved that increased his guilt feelings, something that was probably the reason for his failure to recognize Nora's jealousy: there was an unconscious reason for his making the "honest mistakes that parents make." This was his unconscious hostility.

We feel guilty when we defy authority, whether we are conscious of our defiance or not. Authority may be represented by our parents, teachers, or employers—or the admonitions of childhood which represent to us the right and proper way of doing things. Most people don't show this defiance—which we call hostility—openly. And sometimes they don't even know consciously that they are being hostile.

Now, Nora's father had feelings of guilt based on the hostile feelings he had for her. These feelings were the result of his attitude toward his father. He had always said that his father had been a stern, unpleasant, and forbidding person, that he was rigid and humorless. He always blamed his father for his own unhappiness, not only for his unhappy childhood, but for the troubles which had made him come to a psychoanalyst. Because he was unable to repress his hatred completely (it stayed there, in the back of his mind), it came out in this way: his father was pleased when Nora, the first grandchild, was born; so, by being harsh to his daughter, he would be saying, in effect, that he didn't think much of his father's opinions.

This was only a part of the unconscious expression of hostility; there was another angle: "You were a cruel and ununderstanding parent," he was trying to tell his father. "I am cruel and un-understanding to my daughter, whom you love, in order to give you a taste of what it's like. I want you to suffer the way you made me suffer." This was a futile gesture, like all neurotic hostility, and it was entirely without its intended effect on his father, who would never know that his son was trying to get even with him through Nora.

The unconscious wish to get even with his father, I must hasten to explain, didn't result in his being unkind to Nora *all* the time. He was, by most standards, a good parent. But his reactions to her disobedience were too violent and unreasonable, as if he were waiting for her to give him an excuse, any excuse, to fly off the handle. Also, he and his wife were a little too overjoyed when Freddy was born, and he was somewhat more pointedly fond of the baby than he was of Nora.

From the diminished affection they gave her, and from the amount of affection they showed the baby, Nora could deduce these facts—and, as time went on, amplify them: 1) she was less desirable than Freddy; 2) her parents were right —those infrequent times they said it—she *was* a bad girl; 3) something drastic would have to be done about the baby; 4) her father must not be allowed to think that she would continue to love him, if he didn't love her; 5) she would have to fight hard, to compete, in order to hold her own with her brother; 6) no, that did no good, her father would *never* admit she was better than Freddy; 7) she would have to do *something* to make him love her, or even appreciate her; 8) she would prove to her parents that they were right, that she *was* bad, because it was no use.

Fortunately, when the father began to understand his own problem more clearly, he was able to see how serious was his daughter's problem; she was taken to a psychiatrist and soon an amazing transformation took place. Nora became more lovable. Her father's guilt feelings disappeared when he no longer needed to be hostile, and you can be sure that he appeared more lovable to Nora, too.

Here I want to point out something that isn't often appreciated by parents. Nora's jealousy had started several years before she received any therapeutic help, because her father's attitude forced her to become a seemingly unlovable child. And yet, with help, she was able to reinstate herself in the family as a lovable child and to gain a more wholesome respect for herself as an individual. This shows the potentialities for change in the human personality. Mistakes—even long-standing mistakes—can be rectified. This cannot be repeated too often for parents. In a society such as ours we cannot help but make mistakes, because our patterns of living and bringing up children are changing every day. It is important to know that no difficulties between parents and children are completely hopeless.

Parents get the impression that because they have made mistakes here and there, their children's lives are ruined. As soon as a book appears on the care and feeding, the toilet training, the sex life, the emotional needs of children, mothers and fathers tend to get depressed. Then, when everything is completely out of control and they and their children are utterly miserable, they look for outside help. If things are really wrong, they should go to a psychiatrist at once.

It is rarely the fault of the books; I know that the parents are partially to blame because they misinterpret what the authors say: some people seem to be naturally pessimistic. A writer once said, in one book on infant care, "When a baby is breast-fed, both mother and baby may benefit by it; perhaps the baby develops a feeling of security. But the baby can have feelings of security if he is cuddled when he is given the bottle," etc. Well, there was one young woman being psychoanalyzed who spent a good number of hours accusing herself of being a bad mother. She had read the book I just quoted from, but only parts of it—as a matter of fact, she had only read parts of sentences. Because of physical illness she couldn't nurse her baby, but she felt that she had deprived him of the feelings of security which were rightly his. She had disregarded the words "may" and "perhaps," and she hadn't even begun to consider the author's suggestion about cuddling the infant at bottle time. It didn't matter that she wasn't permitted to nurse the baby because of a breast infection: she had always believed the infection was psychosomatic, that it was caused by an inner dislike of the baby. (She had read somewhere that emotional factors may prevent mothers from nursing their babies.)

As her psychoanalysis soon showed, this mother could have read anything and interpreted it as a reproach: her whole life was consumed with feelings of self-blame. Anything that she talked about was sure to turn out to be derogatory to herself. Obviously she could only read a book on infant care from the points of view that she was *a*) incapable of being an adequate mother, and *b*) here would be the proof of it. (Incidentally, her low self-esteem, it was shown subsequently, was the result of her jealousy of her younger sister, which lasted until her analysis.) But she had one impression of herself which is shared by most parents and it is an almost universal cause for doubting that one is a good parent: she felt she was guilty of neglecting her child. She remembered times when the baby had cried while she was in the shower and couldn't get to him in a hurry. She had repeatedly overslept his 2 A.M. feeding, awakening only when he cried. And there were numberless times she left him in the care of a neighbor while she went to the grocer. As you can see, she was very unrealistic about herself—actually, she was *too* devoted a mother. Overdevotion, over-anything, was very necessary to her. It was the only way she could prove to herself that she was worth while. Her low self-esteem had started in childhood, and now she felt compelled to be a better mother than anyone else in order to convince herself that she was just as *good* as anyone else.

I feel sure that all parents can remember—if they want to—times when they neglected their children, even more than a little bit. Some parents won't admit it, even to themselves; others are only too willing to blame their own "neglect." These are the ones who tend to misinterpret what they read.

These are the parents, too, who are seeking for punishment for what they feel are private sins, and unwittingly they get that punishment from their children. Whatever the child does, whatever he demands, is met with a mixture of self-blame and resignation: "Long ago you needed me and I wasn't there; I deserve recrimination and abuse."

They are not helping the child this way. He only knows that he is not strong enough to solve his difficulties and he finds that his parents are weak and helpless, too. So he resolves his worries by being punitive, for which he is guilty, for which he punishes them some more. Or he demands more and more things, *things* becoming to him the equivalent of love.

As I said before, a child doesn't know what bothers him when he is emotionally upset. Therefore he tries to get release from that bothersome feeling in whatever way he can. But he can go on complaining day after day and demanding things constantly without feeling any better, because the core of the trouble is still there, untouched and unrelieved. This is why so many parents feel that their children are insatiable; they go on treating the isolated signs of disturbance with more ice-cream cones, more toys, and more words, never doing or saying anything that would relieve the true source of the trouble.

Parents who try to assume any blame for the presence of jealousy in their children are wasting their time. In the first place, it will happen anywhere and need not be serious. In the second place, it has been shown by statistics that jealousy as a problem occurs three times more often in families where the mother is overprotective and oversolicitous than in families where the mother neglects her children. The figures were something like this: in families where the mothers were really neglectful, only 26% of the children had definite problems due to jealousy of their brothers or sisters; where the mothers were oversolicitous and overprotective, 80% of the children showed more or less serious symptoms of jealousy. In the so-called normal group, where the mothers were neither neglecting nor overprotecting their children, just about half were having difficulties with the problem.

I am not justifying neglect of one's children; I am only trying to show that if children show jealousy, it is not a sign that they are being neglected. Worse things than jealousy can be seen in neglected children. Exactly why the neglected child is less likely to show his jealousy than the one who is pampered and overprotected is fully discussed in Chapter III; for the present I can offer you this thought: the neglected child felt rejected and unwanted long before the birth of a baby brother or sister; the pampered child gets his *first* push into the cold, cruel world when his mother comes home with a new baby to fuss over. The neglected child, too, usually takes out his feelings away from home, on the playground or on the street.

One will agree that here is a paradox: parents feeling guilty because they *don't* neglect their children, because they are normal parents, because they are aware of their children's problems. "Well," one might say, "that's because they never knew. When it is proved by statistics that jealousy is more prevalent in happy homes than in unhappy ones, that's different. No one will feel guilty then; but it has to be explained to people first." We do explain—psychiatrists explain and explain. Unfortunately, there are too many parents who are so overwhelmed by their personal problems that it affects their appreciation of—and even exaggerates—their children's problems.

Psychiatrists are really a very forgiving group of people. Most of our work seems to consist of trying to get our patients to cultivate a more charitable attitude toward themselves. Ignorance of the law is a good excuse, we think, even if lawyers don't think so. When a mother describes, in greatest detail, her incompetence, blaming herself for the difficulties her children are experiencing, we ask at least this one question: "How could you be expected to act otherwise than you did, if you did not know?" When parents don't know that there is such a problem as jealousy, they shouldn't expect to know how to deal with it; they shouldn't assume that they ought to have known everything about every aspect of being a parent. There is no law that forces people to take a licensing examination that will prove they have mastered all the rules of parenthood. For the simple life, for greater comfort, we can derive some blissful moments from ignorance; I am appealing to those parents who feel that what they don't know hurts them.

Many of the older ideas about children and their problems have changed since I was a boy. It is no longer illegal to pick up your baby when he cries; he is more apt to be spoiled (in the vegetable sense of the word) if you *don't* pick him up. Also, we have discovered that there is no harm in masturbating (handling the genitals) and it has been shown that children who masturbate grow up to be well adjusted and sane. (Actually, the damage which has resulted from masturbation has been the guilt feelings which accompanied it and stayed with the child as he grew older, convincing him he was stupid, or wicked, a potential sex pervert, or a weakling, according to what he was told.) These days many take the position that thumb sucking can be permitted to continue to the age of five, anyway, before it will cause even temporary damage to the teeth.

One can see that even in the science of bringing up babies, things change. To understand children we have to know what it's like to be a child, we have to know what a child needs and how his wants are supplied. It's up to the psychiatrists and psychologists to find out what the child's fundamental needs are, and then it's up to you to see that these needs are satisfied. Child psychology is a complicated study and parents are not expected to know every phase of it by heart; only the essentials ought to be clear to everyone, and these can be boiled down to love, understanding, and protection. When parents are not sure of these simple requirements, when they over-emphasize the few times they have been less than perfect, they will begin to think that their children's problems are the result of their incompetence, and they are in great danger of cultivating guilt feelings. The tendency then is to look for excuses, for alibis, in order to defend themselves. But almost all parents are in the same boat, and the only interest anyone has in their supposed inadequacies is in the amount of time they spend trying to explain them away. Meanwhile, what is going to happen to their children's problems while parents indulge their own?

The answer is, of course, that the children's problems become more complicated because of the parents' problems. When an adult is able to assume responsibility for his own mistakes, it is a most encouraging sign of maturity, assuming he has made mistakes. But more than that, he will not insist on using his own immaturity as a red herring to distract himself from the real business at hand, no matter what it is. He can then say, "I was wrong." He can only say that when he knows where and when he was wrong. Also, he will try to do something about it, and that—especially when dealing with children—is the important thing to do.

A word of explanation is important here. Again and again, and often when least expected, children give their parents the impression of needing something; they seem almost to be carrying signs which read: I HAVE BEEN NEGLECTED, or YOU MAKE ME INSECURE, or WHERE IS THE LOVE, UNDERSTANDING, AND PROTECTION THAT YOU PROMISED ME? These "signs" will seem unreasonable to parents who feel that they have bent over backward to do everything possible for their children. Yet they may blame themselves, recalling a week end when they left the chil-

dren with the neighbors, but brought back gifts for them and
were especially nice to them the rest of the week. The children aren't harping on that, are they? Can they be setting one
week end of seeming neglect against fifty-one week ends this
year, and fifty-two last year, when their parents stayed right
with them?

As a parent one needs all the vitality and objectivity one is
capable of, but chronic guilt feelings, like chronic worry, can
leave one with less energy to cope with the problems at hand.
Therefore, blaming oneself for being "neglectful" is as undesirable as blaming one's children for being "bad." Both of
these are holdovers from theories about human behavior that
we cannot work with constructively.

That is why parents today have such a difficult task before
them. They are trying to create not only happier children, but
also a healthier society, and in the process they will have to
work with new theories, very slowly taking shape now, which
will replace the older, less tenable ones with which we were
brought up.

CHAPTER III

What Causes Jealousy?

———◆———

I N T H E first chapter of this book there is a definition of jealousy which I want to explain more fully: *A child is jealous when he wants something someone else has.* The "something," I explained, was essentially love, understanding, and protection. Why are these things so important? The answer is that the human infant is dependent on his mother for everything he needs, and will continue to remain dependent for a long time to come.

I will be using the various forms of the word "dependency" for the rest of the book, so I shall try to clarify what it means. An infant is a helpless creature, and, in the sense that he has to be helped, he is dependent on his mother. She feeds him because he can't feed himself; he comes to expect that from her: he is dependent on her for food. She protects him. A pin sticks into him and she removes it; she picks him up when he cries, in the middle of the dark nights: he is dependent on her for protection. Along with protection from physical hurt he gets cuddling, a soft voice, the closeness of another human being. All these things we call *love,* because love is inseparable, for a human infant, from the sheer mechanical business of being given food, having diapers changed, and being rocked to sleep.

Therefore, we can say that an infant is dependent on his mother for love, and love for him is narrowed down to the barest essentials. He feels loved when he gets from her whatever he needs: food, being picked up, changed, held, warmed, kissed, relieved of pain, and reassured by the knowledge that she will be there whenever he is uncomfortable. When I say the infant is dependent, I mean this: because he needs all of the things I have talked about and has no way of getting them himself, he has to depend on his mother for them.

A seven-year-old, similarly, is still dependent on his parents for love. He needs less physical protection; they know that he can stand alone, walk, run, roller skate, and climb, and they are confident that he doesn't need to be watched every minute. But he needs psychological protection as much at seven as when he was a baby.

Emotionally, we make growing up very undesirable. For without thinking, most parents will say to a two-year-old: "Don't be a crybaby, you're a big boy now." Or, "You're a big girl; aren't you silly?" (to be afraid of the dark, or to sit on your mother's lap, or to wet your panties).

Most mothers are delighted when the infant starts to crawl or to stand alone, with the same glow of pride as when he first smiled at them when he was fed. But soon they begin thinking about "age norms," and they get uneasy if the baby isn't crawling as early as the book says he should, or if he can't carry on a connected conversation at the age of two. This is an outgrowth of living in a society which stresses achievement and success. We measure success all along the way, beginning very early. We give rewards. There is an extra hug coming to the baby for walking across the room. Or we take away love if success isn't achieved. He gets a look of dismay or reproach if he wets his pants.

But it's no wonder that infancy appears so desirable to so many children. It was the time when everything was synonymous with love: a bottle, being changed, relief of pain, being bathed. That's why we find so many children who want to return to that happy state where they don't have to show A's on a report card, or make any demonstration of being good in order to receive a kiss or a hug. Also, that's why so many adults unconsciously want to go back to the days before they had to accept responsibilities.

You remember David, whom I mentioned in Chapter I. (He

was the seven-year-old who wanted a bottle.) It is obvious that it wasn't hunger which made him ask for the baby's formula. He wanted what it stood for: complete and unconditional acceptance and love, or at least the feeling that they were not being withheld from him. Then why couldn't he have had a bottle? Why, also, couldn't he have sat on his mother's lap and been hugged or read to? Why didn't he and his mother have an interesting conversation about when he was a baby, what he looked like, how funny he was, how helpless and small? Surely parents know how often children need to have said to them: "I love you."

David will go on needing that love for a long time, even while he is growing up and the physical manifestations of love from his mother grow fewer in number. We all go on needing love in adolescence and in adulthood; it becomes a part of mating and sexual maturity when we learn to give love and satisfaction to others. The need for physical contact goes on—we are still mammals—but our infantile needs, when they have been satisfied, are supplanted by more mature needs and more mature expressions of love.

That is why today doctors are so insistent on these important rules: give the infant time to adjust; don't toilet-train too early; don't wean a child too quickly and abruptly. He needs to suck, to be warm, to be held, to be close to a person—an inanimate blanket isn't enough. Parents will find that if they allow him the satisfaction of his infantile needs, he will be ready for sphincter and bladder control in his own good time. He shouldn't be allowed to cry for hours before he is fed; hunger is painful and he needs to be relieved of pain. One should try to ease each new frustration with gentleness. He will gradually learn that he is not going to be abandoned or hurt; he will become secure.

An important question arises: how is it possible, in our culture, to avoid frustrations completely? And will reading this book, plus a hundred other books, teach you how to raise a child so that he will never be frustrated? There is evidence that in other cultures—some of them primitive—children are less frustrated: they aren't weaned until they are three to five years old, nor do they ever leave their mothers' arms, or backs, or bosoms. They are given the most security a child can get, and, it is said, they reach a sort of maturity in their culture which is not too different from the emotional maturity we are trying to achieve in our culture.

Even if this were true, it would be totally impractical for us to try to imitate. The cost is too great. We have spent a number of centuries educating, and thus liberating, women; we accept them, to an encouraging degree, as co-workers with men, on masculine terms. Why, then, should we have to sacrifice these gains by pushing women back into the dull, monotonous drudgery of papoose carrying? Most thinkers on the subject don't feel we have to; it is quite possible to give infants most of the security they need by educating women further, especially by giving parents even greater understanding of infantile needs.

Frustrations of one kind or another are inevitable and universal. Not only do we have to be toilet-trained to live in any group, but we have to observe such things as property rights, and the personal rights of others. We have to learn to live by the rules laid down for us, and within the limits of these rules. If the rules have hampered us we say we are frustrated.

Such frustrations start from the moment the child is born. Perhaps I might be able to make this clearer by discussing a case history—the story of an infant, a normal infant with normal parents. He had no idea that his parents loved him as much as they ever did even when they tried to make him less dependent. He thought they loved him less; he was uneasy because he had no way of knowing that they loved him at the very moment when they seemed to be taking their love away from him.

He had a right to be uneasy and unhappy; he was an infant. Also, he had a right to demand complete, unwavering, and constant attention from his parents: he needed it, and it was only natural that he expected it. After all, he started life by being dependent, and dependency wasn't something he was conscious of. His need to be dependent was an outgrowth of his dependency before birth, when, as an unborn baby, he was the *most* dependent of creatures. He was parasitic, to be exact. Everything he needed was supplied him; without any effort on his part he was fed and he was kept warm.

Then he was literally pushed out into the world. He had to breathe on his own, suck, swallow, get accustomed to the cold, and start his excretion apparatus going. These were all new to him; he never had to do them for himself before, and his birth cry may well have been a protest against the discomfort—the pain, the shock, the cold—which accompanied being born. Actually, he had been getting too big and much too cramped in those quarters, so a change was necessary. All political, social, and economic pessimism aside, this *is* a very difficult world to be born into, no matter how much he wanted to get into it; there were really too many shocks, all at once, for a just-born baby. The first step in growth—being born—was just one painful shock after another.

Remember, he had to leave because he was getting too large for his surroundings, and the only possible good he could derive from forcing himself out was some more space to stretch his limbs, less cramped quarters. He was on his very inadequate and uncomfortable own, and he needed help. He was lucky in one respect: he could get help from his parents, especially from his mother.

In the beginning he was a mass of automatic responses—reflexes. One reflex made him start sucking when his lips were touched: when he sucked he got food. There was another which made him grasp at anything, automatically, when he felt he was falling. When he was too uncomfortable, still another series of reflexes started working: he screwed up his face, did something with his vocal cords, and a cry came out. When that happened, the world around him picked him up, looked for open pins, felt him to see whether he was wet or hot, and gave him something to suck. He was comfortable again. All in all, he was not quite as dependent as he was before he was born, and a little less parasitic.

The first movements he made with his arms and legs may have been just experimental, or accidental, but one day he got his own thumb—or maybe his foot—in his mouth. "What," he very well could have asked himself, "does this remind me of? It's pleasant—it's . . . well, it's like eating!" He had found his first substitute for the nipple. He was not necessarily hungry; his reactions were very simple when he was a few months old. Hunger had been his most constant and unpleasant sensation from the time he was born; eating made the unpleasant sensation very pleasant; eating consisted only of having things put in his mouth; therefore, putting things in the mouth automatically became a pleasant sensation.

His own thumbs and toes were only the beginning. After that came the colored things his parents put in his crib, his aunt's little finger—when she let him—or the edge of his blanket. It got so that he put everything he found in his mouth, or tried to. When they didn't dissolve, and when they were too big to swallow, they stayed there; at least he had *something* in his mouth and, for all he knew, it *might* turn out to be swallowable. Some of the things had to be reached for, not like his thumb, which almost automatically found its way. But those colored beads, for example, had to be reached for, touched, and carried to his mouth, and so reaching for objects, at first only a minor part of the pleasant sensation, came to be a pleasant sensation in itself. His reach was limited by the boundaries of his crib and the length of his arms, as well as his lack of growth and strength, but he was interested in other things around him, even if only for putting-in-the-mouth purposes. This was referred to as "the baby's sense of curiosity," which it was, if you remember that the baby was only curious about how edible things were.

Most impressive was this: whether he knew it or not he had made another move toward independence, in that he was able to find at least one form of satisfaction, or pleasure, by himself. However, the very fact that he had to find it implies that he might not have been getting as much satisfaction as he needed from his mother: it could have been his substitute for the things he wanted from her, which she withheld from him. The most obvious example of this is thumb sucking. It persists in some children, we know, because there is some need for the child to get his satisfactions by himself, because he thinks he cannot depend on his mother, and because he may feel deprived. That is only part of it; sometimes the other elements of the cycle persist. Later on in life, eating too much (putting edible things in the mouth) can make him overweight. This is only one indication of an infantile need which was not satisfied.

What he went through was something like the experience he had when he was born. He gave up that very comfortable prenatal life and became less dependent when he was born. It was not something he wanted because he had heard how nice it was to be born. It was because he had grown too big; he had been quite comfortable there. In much the same way his muscular activity increased because he was growing, and he found —accidentally—how much fun he had sucking his thumb. He could be happy doing something by himself for which he had formerly depended on his mother. The result? He needed her a little bit less; he cried less when he was awake because he found he could amuse himself. But he was picked up less when he didn't cry as much, and that was something he didn't understand.

Being picked up less was a little on the uncomfortable side, because he felt less sure of his mother. To be carried around by his mother had given him the security he needed; part of feeling secure was the knowledge that he would be fed more quickly by being closer to the source of supply. But it also meant protection, and relief of pain, and doing all sorts of things to make him more comfortable. He had come to realize, and expect, that when he was frightened by loud noises and fearful or painful experiences of one sort or another, all he had to do was cry, and she would be there to hold him in her arms and protect him. He also began to learn that when she smiled and made a pleasant noise, and put her face close to his to give him even more protection, he began to feel more

comfortable and secure. In the same way, he learned to
associate no-picking-him-up, or even sudden-putting-him-
down, with displeasure on her part, and this meant lack of
protection.

At any rate, he was slowly becoming aware of the difference
between approval and disapproval. The one was associated
with all sorts of pleasant things: a smile, soft sounds, snuggling,
being picked up and held close: security, or love. Disapproval
appeared often enough to make him unsure of himself: he was
learning that he got disapproval—or less love—as time went on,
for a number of totally unrelated reasons. For example, sometimes his mother showed she was displeased when he cried just
because he wanted to know if she was around. Sometimes he
awoke at three o'clock in the morning; perhaps he cried because it was dark and he was frightened; but no one came to
give him security, or protection, or love.

His need to be dependent on her was increasing, if anything,
but he was slowly becoming aware that she wasn't always there
when he wanted her. She slept away from him—at night, too,
when he needed her most; she left him in his crib (later in
his playpen) when she went around the house doing things.
An infant couldn't possibly have known about his mother's activities; it didn't matter that she was getting food for him, or
cleaning up after him. All he knew was that she wasn't with
him when he wanted her. Well, why wasn't she? Obviously (to
him) it was because she loved him less—he was getting disapproval. If there was to be less love, that meant less food, less
protection, or less security. Disapproval, therefore, helped cause
insecurity: he became worried when she wasn't around.

It is only natural that he would rather have had her approval,
which was smiles, appreciative laughter, kissing, hugging, and
various other signs of affection. These were the rewards for
any part of his behavior that pleased her; because they meant
that he would be held closer, he had the feeling of greater security. The result was that he would repeat over and over again
any acts which had gotten approval before. She would say
"Bang!" and push him over on his back; she laughed and

laughed, then kissed him. She said "Bang!" again and pushed him again. She laughed and kissed him again. Finally he was overwhelmed with affection when he fell over backward by himself after she said "Bang!" It was like a conditioned reflex, wherein he did something and got a certain response, either from himself or from other people, and every time he did the same thing he got the same response. That was how he learned eventually to stop doing things that were disapproved of and to repeat those acts that got him approval.

How this mechanism came to influence his growing up is very impressive and important. He continued to grow stronger and to gain weight, and he learned to crawl. His mother was glad to know he had learned, and proud of his accomplishment. His own motives in learning to crawl went back to the business of eating, and the pleasantness of putting things in his mouth. When he was confined to the crib or playpen, the number of objects he could put in his mouth was naturally limited by the confines of his play area. Outside of this small space there were rooms to explore which, to his mind, seemed tremendous, and full of things to be put in the mouth. Perhaps he felt an increased need for this pleasant sensation because his mother picked him up less frequently; it may have been a substitute for the things she no longer gave him.

Also, when he had to depend on grownups to move him around from place to place, it was never too good. There were lots of corners he wanted to explore; they, too, could have been filled with things to put in his mouth. It was impossible, most of the time, to make the people carrying him understand that. Crawling helped a lot; it not only got him into various places he couldn't be carried to (under tables and chairs), but it turned out to be a cute enough trick for him to get approval, too.

Then there were the things on tables that couldn't be reached from the floor; these things were so far above the floor that he had to stand up to get at them. Because it was a lot of trouble, and because he could see how adults got around much more conveniently by eliminating the business of standing up from a crawling position and then getting down on all fours again, he decided to eliminate this, too. It was hard to do. He had to hold on to things at first, and fall down, and get bumped, but the approval he got from his parents was worth it.

To his way of thinking, approval meant more love, more protection, more security; he had no way of knowing that he was being pushed toward greater independence by being given approval, that when he began to walk he was beginning to walk out of infancy and dependency. Walking was only a trick he had worked up to get places more quickly than he could by crawling, and incidentally to get approval from his mother, as when he first began to crawl. He had no idea of ever leaving her; his need for approval was really further proof of his need to keep on being dependent.

He will eventually live a good part of his life in a series of vicious circles, and this was one of the first. The need to be dependent made him seek the approval of those he was dependent upon, but he was encouraged to do things which made him independent of them: eating by himself and not being fed with a spoon; walking alone and not being carried; learning to read and not being read to; eventually, with full maturity, learning to love and no longer needing only to be loved. It is important to the growing child to be weaned away from infancy; his parents are working in his best interests—and in their own, too.

As nearly as they could make out, he was growing up: he crawled, he walked, he said words that they recognized—so he was ready to advance to the next stage of his growth, childhood. But was he? Was he quite satisfied with leaving infancy? Had he been given all the love and everything else he needed? Was he through being dependent? Leaving dependency behind and learning to be independent would seem to have some advantages: he was getting approval; but he was also giving up something familiar and comfortable—the security of dependency. Why go through with it? What was so important about growing up to be an independent individual?

The goal that he was after, whether he knew it or not, was emotional maturity. This differs from physical maturity in a number of ways, but the most important is that physical development takes place as a growth process naturally, but emotional maturity has to be acquired mostly by learning.

He developed more slowly than other animals because he was a human being. He was an infant—and helpless—for a longer time, but he managed to learn more that way, both intellectually and emotionally. The emotions, drives, and needs of infancy, childhood, puberty, and adolescence are normal for the stages of development in which they occur. They should be left there, or modified, or found to be unsatisfactory for use in the next stages.

Unfortunately, as much as he would have liked to drop them, he was tempted to hold on to previous patterns of behavior because these patterns reminded him of the pleasant sensations of being dependent. It was, therefore, unpleasant to change to increased independence, to grow up, to mature, because he had come to realize that each change carried with it the giving up of pleasant things.

Perhaps this was the result of being weaned too soon, or because his parents expected him to act more like a grownup; they gave him approval as a reward. Physically he advanced to the stage of childhood, but there was some unfinished business which wasn't taken care of when he was still an infant, and the chances were that it would return to haunt him through the succeeding stages of his development. Emotionally he was not ready to be promoted. He may have felt unsure of himself because of the gaps in his emotional life.

An immature adult is a very dependent adult; he is a person still making futile attempts to return to babyhood. His dependency makes it impossible for him to accept the responsibilities of being an adult; he seeks affection because his need for love when he was an infant was not satisfied. He wants to go on living with other adults, but only if he can react to them as if he were still a child.

When he reached childhood, he should have had enough of

the nipple so that he wouldn't have had to suck his thumb; as an adult he should eat to satisfy his hunger, and not because he is still trying to satisfy his need for his mother's love. He was dependent as an infant because he could not do anything for himself. It was only natural to assume that the universe existed for only one purpose: to take care of him. He was the center of it, the most important part of it. Repeated shocks made him give up that idea; he slowly began to realize that there were other people also engaged in living, and that their affairs had less and less to do with his. He had to begin to do more for himself, until there came a point where he had to learn to do things for others.

What might be extremely frustrating for the infant or the child is accepted as necessary by the mature adult, so he meets them emotionally equipped to handle them. To be emotionally mature his desires and satisfactions have to be guided by reality; along with receiving he learns to find satisfaction in giving, too. He has to learn to make his own decisions; he has to learn to do things for and by himself, and not for someone's approval. He has to be able to learn from experience: as a matter of fact, he has to learn how to become emotionally mature from experience, after he finds that magic, wishful thinking, and the expectation that his mother will still help him are utterly useless and childish mechanisms.

It should be obvious that maturity is delayed by any attempt to return to infancy or childhood, which means any attempt to hold on to infant or childhood patterns of behavior. The child could have grown up searching for his lost dependency by trying to find people on whom he could depend. Because he wasn't successful in remaining dependent on his mother, he substituted others for her: clubs, gangs, or just groups of friends. Some people are abnormally dependent on friends and clubs for their security. They are still seeking the love, the security, of infancy.

To complicate a child's life by making him insecure—at the very time he needs security most—helps to delay his growing up. He begins to look for more approval in order to find a substitute for love. He gives up his satisfactions, not because he is ready to, but because he still needs protection and security and is denied his needs to get them. What of these unsatisfied drives, or needs, and the other important parts of his infancy? They are not completely forgotten, even though he doesn't consciously remember them. They stay in the back of his mind, in his unconscious, and there they lie—the memories and desires, the drives to re-experience those very pleasant sensations of infancy; the need to return to childhood, to make up for what he has missed somewhere in the process of growing mature.

For instance, we all know precocious children: they are encouraged in their precocity by their parents, perhaps, or at any rate they are usually children who have been pushed through infancy and childhood. They rarely have a chance to experience to the fullest all the satisfactions they were entitled to have as infants. The result is that they may revolt when their parents least expect it. There is a little girl of seven who wets her bed and sucks her thumb, and was able to read at two and a half. Also, she was trained to the toilet at eighteen months. It was when she became aware that her little brother was enjoying his dependency on her parents that she tried to return to her own babyhood, to re-experience what she had missed. Bed wetting and thumb sucking were not really what she wanted; they were only symbols. The unconscious cannot make its wants known explicitly; it tries to get the individual to return by means of symbols. Bed wetting and thumb sucking stood for infancy, which she had not had enough of, but her efforts were—as are all efforts to return—unsuccessful.

The need to reach emotional maturity, or what I call giving up dependency, is not something the child's parents could have explained to him when he was a child. They could see him growing up and they encouraged him. They were taking credit for his remarkable feats, and never knew that his growth was really a desperate striving for approval, because he had to replace the things he wasn't getting, and which he needed, as an infant. Only when he was entirely through being an infant would he have wanted to grow to childhood. He had no way of knowing that emotional maturity was his goal.

The child was born a sucking infant, because sucking is the exclusive method of eating for all infants. He was naturally dependent on a breast, or a bottle with a breastlike nipple, for his source of food. When he was given a cup or a spoon suddenly, without warning, and the breast or the bottle were permanently removed, what happened to the sucking reflex? That remained dormant because it wasn't being used for getting food, and he could go back to sucking whenever he felt hungry; he could suck his thumb when he needed food or comfort. We know that the sucking reflex is always present; in a person dying of senility, who deteriorates until he has no strength left, the lips will begin to suck again when they are touched, just like a baby's.

All animals who are mammals feed this way, and suckling continues until the young ones can chew their own food or forage for themselves. But the infant of our story was weaned long before that; he was still virtually toothless when they started spoon-feeding him. If, at the time he was weaned, he had been forced to feed himself, he would have starved; he was nowhere near being able to break away from dependency on his mother. By our cultural standards that was proper, because we have come to expect that babies be weaned by the time they are a year old. I should add: whether they are ready for it or not. It is a matter of convenience to wean their young, in humans as well as other animals, but with animals there is this difference: the mothers wait for a shorter period of time because in that shorter period their young have developed more fully than human infants do in a longer period.

A lion cub is dependent on his mother until he has grown to the point where he is too big to suckle and requires more milk than she can give him; when that happens she begins to see that it is time to stop nursing him. It's easier to let him share her food, and he is permitted to hunt with her, until he begins to eat too much. Then he is growled at and soon realizes that he may as well begin looking for his own food.

This isn't cruelty that the animals show; the mothers know that their cubs can take care of themselves. They will continue to protect them from other animals until the youngsters turn into rivals for their food, and then they are on their own for good.

But are they? In the sense that they band together for protection, we could almost assume that animals are dependent creatures, and they grow to adulthood to travel in packs, herds, or flocks. When puppies are taken from the litter too soon they are much more attached to (dependent on) their human masters than those that stay longer in their litters; they don't need to run in packs and are more the devoted pets you hear about. Usually, though, when an animal forages for his own food it should be remembered that he is good and ready to be on his own, physically.

I don't know where our parents, or their ancestors before them, first got the idea that a child could be weaned while he was still an infant. Offhand I can think of one explanation: some of them, long ago, may have become impatient with the length of time it takes for a baby to get over being an infant. They may have been influenced by the animals around them. Dogs, cats, cows, and horses seem to pass through infancy and childhood in no time at all, and are fully grown in the same number of months it takes a human infant to learn to walk. Human infancy is a long-drawn-out process, by any standards. Humans take longer to reach adulthood than most animals, especially the domestic animals; but they will live longer, and can have children over a longer period of time; they are more highly specialized physically and mentally, and it *should* take longer to develop all these processes.

The infant we have been discussing is a fairly normal youngster. Can we say that he will be secure, that he won't have to worry about his status? I don't think so; it isn't so easy. If his mother has tried to ease his frustrations, to heal their sting with love, he will learn gradually to accept his parents' mode of living and will become a social human being. He is going to live in a society where we have rules to regulate mealtimes,

playtimes, and love-making. To develop control will be easy
when he is permitted to grow up slowly. He will then grow
up emotionally, in rhythm with his muscular growth and his
ability to reason.

At times he will feel that his mother is an inconsistent and
inconsiderate person. She leaves him feeling loved at one time
and unhappy at another time. As an infant, he makes many
demands on his parents. Those demands are not all obvious,
and even his obvious demands are not too easy to cope with,
when one considers the number of times he cries and the attempts he makes to get off the feeding schedule, as well as all
the other signs of physical discomfort which seem to have been
designed by nature to awaken his parents to their responsibility for taking care of him.

That is why, with all the attention he got from his parents,
he felt worried when another baby arrived. To the child it
meant loss of love. He felt disapproved of; he was angry at his
parents for not loving him any more; it left him feeling lost,
frustrated, and helpless, and wondering what it was he had
done to displease them.

If he showed his disapproval openly he might have been punished, which meant even more loss of approval; the alternatives were better. He could take it out on the baby, or hide it
from everybody, including himself. We call this "inhibiting,"
or repressing, his true feelings. Although showing his dislike
for the baby might mean disapproval, it had this advantage:
they might get rid of the baby if they saw how upset he was,
or take it back where it came from; or it might disappear; and
he would be the center of everything again.

If he decided to inhibit his resentment of his parents he
did it not only because there was loss of approval involved, but
also because one just doesn't go around hating one's parents.
(It isn't hard to get to learn what behavior is expected of one.)
Hate wasn't a very worthy emotion. More than that, it wasn't
very pleasant, because it helped confirm his suspicion that perhaps he really was a bad child. (That, by the way, was one of
the things he thought of when he was wondering what was

wrong with him that made his parents love him less.) He was reluctant to think about himself as a bad child—who wouldn't be?—and so he had another reason not to show it. When he inhibited his resentment against the baby and devoted himself to it he got more approval; they might even have complimented him for being such a good child. He might have liked that—anything to offset his feeling that perhaps he wasn't a good child.

Whatever the reason for not showing his dislike of his parents and the baby, merely inhibiting the emotion didn't make it disappear forever. That feeling, too, was stored in the part of the mind we call the unconscious, where he stored all such unpleasant, unworthy, and disagreeable thoughts, and there it would remain unremembered by the conscious mind, but trying always to come out. Custom, training, or habit made it rather difficult for him to hate his parents openly, no matter what his unconscious demanded. His hidden hostility could have been directed toward his parents in such a way that neither he nor they recognized it as hatred. Years later this unconscious resentment might still influence his behavior toward his wife, his own children, his boss, or the people he works with.

His jealousy toward an older brother or sister could have come about in almost the same way. He would have to find someone to blame for being deprived of the affection he demanded, and which he was not getting. Perhaps he looked around him and saw an older child usurping part of his own personal universe. It wouldn't matter that the older child could be just as jealous of him, that the older child may have had more reason to be jealous.

I have tried to show how the infant starts out as a dependent and resents the loss of whatever he has enjoyed in his dependency. But, as I have pointed out, the growing child can and will become more and more independent, if he is given the necessary help and reassurance.

Jealousy arises naturally out of this dependence and the feeling of being deprived by someone else. In families where there are boys and girls the same things happen. The boys need very little evidence that their sisters are getting more than they do, and the girls can point to dozens of incidents each day to prove that boys have all the fun. There is also the matter of penis envy, which Freud first described. It isn't necessarily sexual, although it may be. It means just what it says: A little girl sees that her brother has a penis and she envies him. He has something she doesn't have, and this is, you will remember, our definition of jealousy. Penis envy can be the sole cause of jealousy between brothers and sisters, but more often the feeling occurs in addition to other feelings of deprivation.

Penis envy occurs in boys, too. Sometimes it is the feeling that their sisters have something they do not have—no penis; and sometimes it is envy of an older brother who has a larger penis. (This could also be envy of the father's penis or any other differences in body contour that either a boy or a girl may detect in another member of the family.) Sometimes a little boy who is jealous of his sister will conceal his penis between his thighs and walk around saying, "Look! I'm a girl, too." It isn't at all uncommon to find children in some aboriginal groups (where jealousy of older boys is part of the tribal custom) who, by hand or by mechanical devices, try to stretch their penises and make them longer. All of these things are attempts to get something that someone else has.

If one has any notion that these problems don't arise when the mother is seemingly more devoted, it would be good to see what happens to the children of an overprotective mother. Such a mother thinks she is giving her child everything he needs—she may even nurse him for a year or two—but something is always missing, mostly because she is indulging herself and not him. She gets satisfaction out of his dependency and helplessness, which makes her feel important. She loves him only because she wants *him* to love *her,* and this emphasizes his need to be dependent on her. But then she thwarts him. When he starts to crawl and when he starts to walk, he is stopped dead in his tracks: "Because," the mother says, proud of her interference, "he may hurt himself." She frustrates his attempts to eat things he finds on the floor, she doesn't allow him to be near other children ("Germs, you know"), and when he grows a little older, to childhood, when he wants to play with other children his age, she won't let him ("They are too rough," or dirty, or profane, or they are bad examples). So it goes: he is frustrated as an infant in his need for dependency and further frustrated when he tries to be independent.

The behavior of the overprotective mother is even more inconsistent than that of the ordinarily devoted and normally protective mother. But mother and child eventually become accustomed to their relationship, and he may remain a mama's boy for too long, even as an adult.

Such a child will resent even more than usual the arrival of a new baby, because he has everything to lose; not only the natural, normal dependency that children show, but the dependency that was forced on him by his mother. He has no resources of his own—no independence—and no way of life away from his mother. The arrival of a new baby is a terrible blow to him, so he can only look on it as complete and absolute desertion. His resentment or jealousy of the new baby is very impressive. The children of oversolicitous mothers have a harder time with jealousy than any other children.

The overprotective mother is frequently found in a family group consisting of husband, wife, and only one child. The dependent only child may become jealous of his father, who, he feels, is taking up too much of his mother's time. The Oedipus complex, which we discussed earlier, describes what happens in such situations.

Parents can do many other things which are prone to arouse greater feelings of jealousy between their children. There are some racial and religious groups, for example, which favor the sons in the family, especially the first-born son. Obviously the other children will be jealous of him, while the daughters will be jealous of their brothers' extra privileges and other signs of favoritism.

The point I want to make here is this: we have known for some time that the approach to the problem of how to bring up children should change, and the change has been toward more care, more affection, and with greater regard to the infant's demands. From the things I have said, it is quite possible to infer that children are being brought up in such a way that they feel insecure. As a result, they will resent any intrusion which would threaten to make them feel even more insecure. For this reason there has to be jealousy wherever there are brothers and sisters in the same family. Jealousy is normal in our society for too many reasons over which we have no control.

I have tried to point out the possibilities that the reason for insecurity in our children is that we have tried to make them more independent too soon, whereas their need is to be more dependent, and for a longer time. If the child's needs could be completely satisfied, he would not be insecure and he would grow emotionally. We must face the fact that we are not satisfying our children's needs as completely as perhaps they want, but I want to remind parents that the way most parents bring up their children is the only possible way of bringing them up in this culture, surrounded by the economic and social factors of our life. If parents would think a moment of all the steps that would have to be taken to prevent any worries at all in their children, they would see how awesome a task they would face.

When I refer to insecure people, the people who eventually go to a psychiatrist for help, I mean those who spend their whole lives seeking the dependency of infancy. These are the emotionally immature people. In their jobs they cannot feel competent unless they are given constant reassurance; they resent their bosses, just as they once resented their teachers, and for the same reason: the slightest criticism means that they are not loved. They feel unloved, so they may become abnormally promiscuous, or alcoholic, or cruel. Their emotional life is that of the infant, and the normal frustrations of life appear as they would to an infant—insurmountable and threatening. They still carry around with them the unsatisfied needs of childhood. Perhaps they were not allowed to express these needs openly—they may even have been punished for making normal demands on their parents. They eventually take one of two alternatives: some become overly submissive, too willing to believe themselves inadequate, while others become overly aggressive, too demanding of their (to them) rights. In either case they have disguised their true feelings by replacing them with anxiety, feelings of guilt, or hatred.

The secure child lives in a world where there are shocks. They may shake him a little, worry him, frighten him—make him a little less sure and somewhat unhappy—but if he knows that he is loved and protected, he will be basically secure. The secret of emotional growth lies in this: at some point in his growing up, armed with his security, he will learn to withstand the shocks and frustrations of childhood, adolescent, and adult living. He has to learn to face living in this world without the infantile need to expect that his mother, or magic, or his psychoanalyst—or any other substitute for his mother—will smooth the rough spots, or ease his pain, or soothe him with "Of course I love you. Now do you feel better?"

I have tried to show what we have learned so far from research in child development, from the study of normal people, and from treating those who are emotionally sick. I want to point out what parents can do, what parents can expect, and what limitations there are. We cannot step out of our culture and create the impossible. You can be a good parent even though you have difficulties with your children, if you hold on to your faith in yourself and in your children. And, when you need assistance, you can have faith, too, in the doctors and psychologists who are studying children constantly, and who can help by showing us how and why we come by our feelings.

CHAPTER IV

Spoil the Child and Spare Your Rod

I N T H E last decade there have been many books written trying to convince parents and teachers that they ought to be kind and gentle with children. There is distinct need for such books. Too many parents don't want to give in to their children; they say: "I don't want my child to grow up feeling that everyone around him is going to wait on him." Or, they are afraid to reassure the jealous child; they think he might take that as a signal to be more destructive or more hostile.

The goals parents have set for themselves and their children are not so bad, but the means they use in achieving those goals are often self-defeating. Parents have been afraid to love their children enough because they were afraid that affection would make youngsters grasping or antisocial. Actually, they were not afraid of their children as much as they were afraid of their own emotions.

There is nothing wrong with humanity except the way it is treated, and there is nothing wrong with an infant except what may be done to him by his parents and others who are taking care of him. In this chapter I want to assure parents that permissiveness and gentleness will help them reach their goals more surely than deprivation and punishment.

If we take a look at the world itself and see what is happening to the people in it today, we may want to agree with those psychiatrists who say that this world of ours has on a sickly smile while it is trying to be brave. A sick world suffers from mental troubles that may not be serious enough to call for hospital care, but troubles which can be avoided by preventive measures. Most neuroses (the mild forms of mental illness) and some psychoses (the serious forms that need to be hospitalized) can be prevented by proper mental hygiene. Mental illness itself can be defined most simply as the difficulties people have in their inter-personal relations.

If a child has difficulties in his relationships with his parents, the chances are that he will grow up having difficulties in his relationships with other people. If the trouble he has as a child can be taken care of when he is young, it will help him so that he will be able to deal with people on a more pleasant basis later on in life.

Take the case of Louise Hanks, who went to an analyst because she was troubled about the sexual side of her married life. She had married a man who, while he wasn't old enough to be her father, was certainly sedate and conservative enough. The story of her life showed this pattern of behavior: her favorite teachers throughout school and college were the fatherly type; when she went to work, her bosses were men in their fifties or older. Ordinarily this in itself would not have been unusual, except that she had given up a number of rather good jobs because she couldn't get along with men her own age. She resented working for anyone less than twenty years older than she, and would resign from job after job because of her own admitted unpleasantness. She once told her psychoanalyst that she thought he was fifty-two years old, although he was really thirty-eight. This sort of distortion is common: while an analyst may be fiftyish to some, other patients will think of him as thirty-odd or even younger, and sometimes too young to be trusted with their problems.

To get back to Louise: she distorted the personalities of the men she came into contact with because she was always on the lookout for a father. Her mother died when she was six. She was the youngest and her mother's favorite. Her two older sisters were her father's favorites. She was never able to get the exclusive attention of her father, but she never stopped trying. She flattered him and was certainly more affectionate toward him than her sisters were. She admired and respected him, and this admiration and respect was eventually pinned on all men who were old enough to be her father.

Louise's devotion to her father did not need to become abnormal. Mental hygiene at the time of her mother's death, when her competition for her father and her jealousy of her two sisters began, could have stopped her from carrying out her childhood desires after she had become an adult. In other words, preventive measures could have made her better equipped to get along with people. However, it would have taken a more understanding father to have seen to it that his daughter had psychiatric help.

Almost every little girl at some time has a crush on her father. But, as she grows to adolescence, she is drawn toward boys her own age, and gradually her father will begin to seem old and fussy indeed! She is following a normal growth pattern; she takes her father's admiration for granted and we can hope that in her future life she won't have to look for fatherly love in other men.

We also hear about the type of father who is a stern disciplinarian, usually as a result of having been a strictly disciplined child himself. This is the father who was brought up in that school of thought which held that it is good for infants to "learn to suffer" at an early age. I don't know if they felt that the child would be able to suffer *better* when he grew up or if he would be able to suffer *quicker* due to his early training. These are possibilities. They were, in fact, the more likely result of such a father's actions. The same school of thought held to the strictest sort of discipline in every aspect of bringing up the child: toilet training to be completed at ten months or a year, never picking up the child when it cries (only when there is a fire), never giving an inch, never smiling, never playing with the baby, and never giving it any love at all. The result was a very rigid individual who grew up easy to train; he preferred a regimented form of life; he would have thrived in a dictatorship.

He had to. From the time he was born he was punished for every attempt to express an individual idea, even if it was only a cry of hunger. Every attempt to break away from the pattern his father had set down for him was met with blows, either physical or verbal, and he got used to the idea that it was less painful physically and mentally to obey the orders of someone in charge. At first it was his father, later on it was his teachers, and still later his commanding officers. If it were possible to get opposing armies made up only of these rigidly trained people, they would soon kill each other off in the same unreasoning, blindly-devoted-to-duty way in which they were trained to tackle every problem that ever arose. Then the rest of us who are left could give in to our children, delay their toilet training until they are ready for it, and bring up a very healthy, peace-loving, tolerant new world.

Take the question of early weaning. Judging by the effect it has had on children until now, and looking at the behavior of other animals (I have mentioned that all mammals except humans nurse their young until they are able to go out and forage for themselves), it might occur to us that we are weaning our children too soon. If so, why not change our thinking and our habits so that mothers will nurse children for a longer period of time? If they are incapable of supplying them with milk, their children could be bottle-fed, but, as we said before, held in their mothers' arms when they are given the bottle. In this way the baby gratifies his sucking impulse and feels the comfortable closeness of his mother. But early weaning is not the only mistake we make in bringing up our children.

Most parents want to pick up their children when they cry and give in to their demands, but they have been harassed by old wives' tales about spoiling the baby. Unfortunately, these were reinforced during the last few generations, when some of the most vicious propaganda against children was started. If parents listened to the *old* old wives they would learn that it wasn't too unusual to nurse a baby for two years and that it was considered normal to stay with one's child for most of the day, and above all they would learn that children weren't spoiled by this kind of attention.

Well, it doesn't spoil an infant to give him more security, nor does it spoil an infant if he is given so many of the things he wants that he rarely cries. After all, he only cries because he wants something. If he doesn't get what he wants when he wants it, he becomes worried. If he worries that he won't get what he wants, he becomes afraid and insecure. He is insecure when he is not sure of himself and when he is not sure if others will help him. He becomes anxious. (In psychiatric usage, the word "anxiety" means *worry* about the *fear* of *insecurity*.)

When a child has no fear, he can trust himself on those (to us) dangerous steps to independence. He grows up emotionally when he doesn't *have* to have approval, when he doesn't need substitutes for his mother's breast. When he isn't afraid, he tries things out. He finds decided advantages in giving up some of his dependency needs. He doesn't have to be pushed into independence; he discovers by himself that it is more comfortable and interesting to be independent.

With all the overwhelming evidence that children need more than we have been giving them, there comes the question: what made us stop giving? (It seems that there was a time when mothers devoted themselves more completely to their children.)

One explanation is that our parents may have considered it peasantlike to nurse a baby or to spend a good deal of the time with it. Mothers tried to get away from doing things that would seem unenlightened, uncultured. And they justified the change with remarks like these:

"What if he does cry? All babies cry." That's true. All babies cry when they want something, whether it is food, or affection, or relief from pain.

"If you pick him up every time he cries, he will know you are giving in to him." That's true, too. He is crying because he wants you to pick him up. It is the only way he can tell you that he needs you. He expects you to give in to him, which is why he cries.

"I'm sure you don't want to have to devote your whole life

to bringing up your baby." This is true, too. Few mothers really want to devote their entire lives to the bringing up of their babies.

"If you pick him up every time he cries he will be spoiled." This is *not* true. It is only true if he has had to cry so long and so loudly each time he needs something that he doesn't dare leave the maternal arms without protest, for fear he will never be picked up again!

When women began to approach equality with men, they sought jobs away from the home and left the work of baby tending and housekeeping to others. These women would have been the first to want to believe that the infant shouldn't be picked up. They probably felt guilty and afraid: guilty of not giving their children enough care, and afraid that their children would grow up to be problems.

Women in business and industry had less time to spend with an infant. The latest ideas about rearing children and the newer ideas about womanhood seemed to be compatible. It followed logically, then, that the professional groups agreed that babies shouldn't be picked up when they cried. The "habit-training" schools of psychology fell in very neatly with the newer status of women. Habit training meant that you treated the child as though he were an automaton without emotional responses. You were supposed to let him cry and cry and finally he'd learn not to cry. He learned it, but bitterly.

Doctors gave parents schedules of when to feed infants which had nothing to do with the individual baby's rate of digestion, or the amount of food he needed. Some parents may have cheated a little on scheduling but, on the whole, they had faith in their doctors. They were fortified by current popular beliefs and their babies were given food according to the clock, or picked up only to be changed. Baby's formula was sterile and nourishing. Mothers felt efficient when infants gained weight, when they kept themselves clean, and when they themselves had more time for their own work or professional careers. Meanwhile, what had happened to the infant's feelings? Was his mother really any happier and was parenthood more satisfying?

We know that it was not the answer, for maladjustment and discontent did not disappear. Mothers were now not only parents, but also responsible citizens, efficient managers, charming hostesses, and trim-looking wives. They had to be well informed and well groomed in order to keep up with unmarried women in the career world. It was a larger job than women had ever taken on themselves before; if they weren't successful it was only because doing two jobs is sometimes impossible. But we know now that to be a good mother a woman must have a life of her own, as well as a life she lives for her children. The one is part of the other; the two lives are lived together if the best in womanhood is to emerge. When that happens, you can be sure that it will be the best possible life for her children, too.

The most difficult part of this dual existence is in knowing what proportions of her life a mother should allot to herself and to motherhood. The answer isn't easy to give. Knowing how much care an infant needs, it would be hard to say that a mother could have any time at all for herself. But this much can be said: a mother who goes about her own life before the baby has had a chance to be as dependent on her as he has wanted to be, isn't fair to the baby. What's more, she isn't going to like herself when he shows her how insecure she has helped him become.

The change in women's status is only one thing; the idea that babies shouldn't be picked up lest they be spoiled is another. They are only a small part of the many factors involved in achieving mental health for the individual and, perhaps, for society. The question of mental health is, after all, international. We know that an improvement in the mental health of the world is needed. We are a suffering, uncomfortable, unhappy, and anxious world. I think that has been quite well established. One reason might well be that the individual is neglected in favor of efficiency. It's more efficient to standardize the way people are brought up and live. Outside of some minor changes here and there, and except for a few groups of people, you will find that all of us are brought up pretty much the same, in this sense: the individual has to fit into the scheme of things, so he conforms to standard operating procedure. Because it's easier, the temptation is to stick to the rules and regulations as much as possible.

For example, there are laws to make children go to school at a certain age. Now I am not opposed to sending children to school, nor am I opposed to the other rules and regulations we live under. It *is* more efficient, and by and large most of us can live fairly happily in what is called a well-ordered existence. However, I feel, as I think most psychiatrists do, that extreme forms of regimentation can destroy individuality altogether, and this is the efficient but vicious procedure which is followed in a dictatorship.

Too many people think that the world has a way of correcting its mistakes by itself. This smacks of magic. The changes come about by propaganda, which, depending on the individual or group putting it out, can be good or bad. In general, we can say that most bad government comes from unhappy, insecure leaders appealing to an unhappy, immature people. It isn't hard to show that the worries and discomforts of adults can be traced to their worries and discomforts as infants. Therefore, it would seem reasonable to suppose that if you brought up an infant entirely free from worry—I mean *entirely* and not partially—you would be able to produce a more mentally healthy adult than we find around us today. If one mentally healthy adult can reach emotional maturity by being brought up feeling so secure, it's possible that a whole nation could be brought up the same way.

To convince people that an improvement in the world's mental health is needed, and that the approach is primarily by the way of better child care, is a most stupendous task. However, this isn't a mentally healthy world when it is filled with unhappy people, wars, suffering, and atomic bombs, so some sort of change is needed. (It may mean that parents will have to adjust themselves emotionally to their children with greater intensity than they do now. They may have to undertake greater responsibilities toward them. It may mean that parents will tie their social lives into what may appear to be highly uncomfortable knots.)

Of course, there's always the question as to whether or not it can be proved that a new plan will work. Some psychiatrists think that there is proof, and they point to other cultures and other civilizations where the approach to child care is different from ours. Studies of primitive and aboriginal society have been going on for some years. (Next to the study of the psychology of children, I think that studying sociology, the history of society, and anthropology, the development of peoples, are most important in the training of a psychoanalyst.) It might be interesting to see how people elsewhere in the world handle the problem of bringing up their children.

An interesting report was made by some navy psychiatrists who were on the island of Okinawa during World War II. Despite the lack of some of the advantages of civilization that we have grown used to, and despite their very obviously lower standards of living, the Okinawans are quite mature emotionally, even by our definition of emotional maturity. They behave in some ways that we would deplore, but this behavior is their very realistic approach to everyday problems. Among other things in their favor is this: for some 450,000 people there isn't a single mental hospital, and they don't seem to need any. This isn't because they are too uncivilized; they have a rather well-developed civilization which is somewhat less mechanical than ours; at any rate, they are not savages or aborigines. The most serious mental illness seen there was usually the result of brain damage, when it happened because of disease or injury. Even then there were only about fifty such persons in one community of 48,000 people. For another thing, those physical diseases we find so prevalent in the western world, and which are largely brought about by "nervousness" (there are a great number of them), are exceedingly rare. Some of them don't even exist, despite the fact that their ideas of personal hygiene are far below our standards.

In many less-civilized groups the baby is nursed for a very long time due to economic necessity: they don't know about formulas and bottles, so they are forced to feed the child at the breast. Some of the aborigines go through this very healthy —for the child—procedure, but add to it a whole series of rituals based on superstition. For instance, sometimes we find that the mother is separated from the rest of the tribe and is unapproachable by her husband for two years after the baby is born. This is presumably done so that she won't have another baby to nurse—who might deprive the older child of his food. Although the baby gets all this protection and love and food —and these things could be so helpful in making him mentally healthy—they have rituals to make the baby learn fear at a very early age, and the mothers go out of their way to develop jealousies between their children.

But the Okinawans seem to have a better understanding of how children should be brought up. The mother nurses her child until he is three years old or even older; he is carried on her back and she never leaves him. The instant he becomes hungry, he is fed. These people have a very superior understanding of the value of breast feeding. The mother's milk may be gone and the child may no longer need to be breast-fed, but when he begins to show signs of fear or worry he is given a breast to suck on, sometimes even his grandmother's, and he is quiet and contented again.

The reports state that there are no spoiled or problem children, nor are they over-dependent. Toilet training doesn't begin until the child is three or four years of age, by which time he prefers to imitate older children; he isn't forced into training, and he is never punished. Bed wetting is treated as an illness; the treatment is crude and—to us—brutal: they place burning leaves against the child's skin. The child has been taught this is treatment for an illness and not punishment, so the bed wetting gradually decreases, exactly as if he were recovering from an illness. Probably what happens is that

the child isn't blamed for the bed wetting, any more than
we would blame a child for having mumps. He doesn't feel
bad or inadequate. Besides, he sees other children receiving
the same treatment, just as our children know that their
friends have measles, chicken pox, and colds, or sometimes
get painful inoculations or take disagreeable medicines.

The children of Okinawa are not over-dependent. It is important to emphasize this because we have been told that our
children would become over-dependent if we let them nurse
too long or if we gave in to them too much. It has always been
assumed that over-dependence is the result of getting used
to dependency and wanting it forever. Apparently it isn't
that at all; over-dependence is the result of not having experienced enough dependence when the child needs it most,
when he is an infant, so that his goal for the rest of his life is
to be a dependent person, to experience what he missed in
his infancy.

The child who is breast-fed for a comparatively long time
will eventually find out that it is more convenient to leave
his mother's breast and find his own food. Waiting around
for her to feed him gets to be too much trouble after he is
able to walk; it means that he has to interrupt his games
with the other children and start looking for his mother
when he is hungry. There are other advantages in leaving his
mother's breast. He can get a greater variety of food when he
wants it; also, leaving his mother means having greater freedom. The child, then, grows independent of his mother only
when he finds out that he can get more by being independent,
and not because he can get approval. After all, isn't it just
about all the approval in the world when a mother lets her
child be as dependent on her as he wants to be?

The Okinawan child is never separated from his mother
during the first three to five years of his life. Some of our men
who were stationed there tried to help out the women by offering to hold their babies, or by making cribs for them. They
felt that the mothers worked too hard, that it would be only
decent to relieve them of their burdens. They were shocked

and startled at the reaction. The moment the baby was separated from his mother he would cry. This was more impressive because the sound of a baby crying was so very unusual. The babies are never so far from their mothers that they miss them, and they were naturally upset by any separation. Of course your mother was devoted, too, according to our standards, and in keeping with the customs of our times. If she had been able to carry you around on her back all the time, and had never left you in your crib alone, you would never have had to cry either—and your mother would have been laughed at by the neighbors. The native baby felt insecure only on those few occasions when he was separated from his mother. Your moments of insecurity were more frequent than his.

Again the question arises: did our childhood experiences with so much insecurity make us better equipped to handle insecurity when it occurred later in life? Does the Okinawa baby suffer permanent damage the few times he feels insecure? Or does his constant feeling of security make him better equipped to handle insecurity when he grows up? The Okinawa baby is probably stronger psychologically because he never had to feel insecure, and he is therefore better able to handle his problems.

Furthermore, he is not rushed through infancy. He is accepted as an infant, his infant prerogatives and privileges are respected, and only when he is quite finished with infancy does he go on to the next stage of growth. By that time he is ready and very willing to leave behind him infantile patterns of behavior. They would only hamper him in his childhood and later.

To sum up the main differences in the way the Okinawans bring up their children and the way we do: Okinawan women spend more time with their children, carry them around on their backs while they work, and nurse them for three or more years. They have learned to recognize and accept all these responsibilities toward their children, and they are quite willing to carry them out. Frankly, I think it would be utterly preposterous for us to assume that the Okinawans or any others have the only answer. I haven't brought up the subject of child care in the Pacific because I am in favor of their way of doing things, but only to show you what some others are doing elsewhere, without formulas or rigid feeding schedules.

We are not hopelessly lost because we were brought up in a way that leaves a lot to be desired. We do have fun, and many of us reach happiness in spite of our early difficulties. There are two reasons which come to mind and which may help you understand how hopeful the situation really is. For one thing, usually we learn how to find substitutes for things we think we have missed and for the things we have really missed. The civilization which has caused so many changes in our way of living also helps to provide many satisfactory, or almost satisfactory, diversions. At least, they are not always attempts to recapture what we missed as infants. The second point is this: parents usually try to compensate for some of the things their children miss. When they can make up to their children for some of the things that have happened, it helps to ease what could otherwise turn out to be serious mutual difficulties.

As children or as adults, we can always use a little better understanding of our problems by those around us; that's why one should never say, "I have not been a good parent. I have ruined my child's life. There is just nothing that can be done about it." The important thing to remember is that it is never too late for parents to cultivate an understanding of themselves and of their children, nor is it too late to catch up on some of the things they have neglected before. Even if they have made the most horrible mistakes in the world and their children are the scourge of the neighborhood, there is still time for them to do something about it; if the problem seems too big for them to handle, they can get outside help. Psychiatrists and child-guidance clinics are better equipped than they are to handle the more serious problems in their family. As time goes on, we find that parents are less ashamed to admit that they or their children need psychiatric help, and this is a most encouraging sign.

I'm not advocating the development of a crew of willful, disobedient, and vicious brats whose behavior is unbridled and undisciplined. You will find, if you look carefully enough, that such children act this way as a revolt against the mistakes their parents have made. The parents may become stricter in their discipline, but the little devils will bounce back and behave even worse, if possible, than before. When it becomes a matter of who will break down first, the parents or the children, the odds are in favor of the children to win every time. The reason is simple: the children's behavior is the result of their parents' mistakes; the parents don't know that they have made mistakes, and the chances are that they won't know in the future, either, without outside help.

There was one mother who decided that before she began to spank her six-year-old boy, Tommy, she ought to go to a clinic for advice. Tommy was a distinct behavior problem in school and in the neighborhood; the children's mothers hated and were afraid of him, and disliked her. Living there had become very uncomfortable. Tommy scratched, bit, threw stones, and mauled other children and adults. His kindergarten teacher told the principal that her shins were a mass of bruises; she said she was going to resign if she weren't allowed to take at least one good healthy smack at Tommy once a day, until he cut it out. The principal had a heart-to-heart talk with Tommy's mother, which was when she decided that she ought to get help.

His mother said that he really loved his baby brother, who was then about a year old. His father was in the army during the war and she had to work during the day, so he was taken care of by a combination maid, cook, and nurse from the time he was about seven months old. She thought that he may have cried more than other children did at night, until he was about two; although at that time she never went out evenings but stayed home. She remembered that it was very hard to wean him from the bottle; his digestion was bad, he lost weight, and he was sickly. He sucked his thumb until he was four and a half.

She was asked, "Did he want to try the bottle again after the baby was born?"

"Why, yes," his mother said. "I was very embarrassed at first, but I let him have it when his father wasn't around. My husband would have been furious with me if he had known Tommy wanted to drink water or milk out of a bottle once in a while."

"Children frequently start on the bottle again when another child is born," she was told. "Tommy did it after you had trouble weaning him, and because he sucked his thumb; those are pretty good signs that he didn't have enough nursing. He might have wanted the bottle a long time before, and he only had nerve enough to ask when he saw the baby have one. Jealousy of the baby makes him want what the baby has."

"But Tommy isn't jealous," his mother said. "He really loves his little brother."

With Tommy's background of so many things which made him insecure, it was natural that he would show resentment when anything happened to increase his insecurity. However, he found it to his advantage not to take out his resentment on the baby. Because it had to come out somehow, he directed it against the other children and the grownups around him. We expect children to be aggressive when there is a new baby; some of them show it toward the baby, others toward their parents, while still others hide it completely inside of them, only to have it come up later on when they are prodded by their unconscious.

Tommy's mother was reassured that he wasn't going to grow up to be a criminal, but that she needed help with the problem of his fighting. If she punished him when he hit people he would be convinced that his parents disapproved of him. He would have to assume that they disapproved of him because he was a bad boy. Children always blame themselves when they don't get approval. They know they get it when they are extra-good. When they get disapproval, they think it must be because they are extra-bad. Punishing Tommy would have increased his very bad opinion of himself, it would have made him feel even more guilty, and it would have increased his resentment against his baby brother. If his resentment increased, he would undoubtedly become more vicious toward others. It would be important, first, to try to keep him from hitting anyone; second, to convince him that he was still loved; and third, to assure him that he was not a bad boy.

This was done through his mother and his teacher. Tommy was given new games to play, books, and more responsibility both at home and in school, the aim being to divert him from his aggressive ideas. He didn't become less aggressive overnight, but he was watched carefully and whenever possible he was prevented from hitting anyone. As it turned out, this last was exactly what he wanted: to be *stopped* from being bad. After all, he didn't *want* to be bad; he would rather have been good because he wanted approval. But he wasn't able to control his temper. Children should not be expected to have as much self-control as adults; they don't know that they lack it, and so they can't understand why they are bad. All they know is that they *are* bad. That's why they are extremely grateful to anyone who helps keep them in check.

Unfortunately, Tommy's aggressiveness continued to crop up when his mother wasn't around and there were too many times when the poor boy just *had* to sock something—anything. Because his mother and his teacher realized this and because they would rather have him sock some*thing* than some*body*, he was encouraged to get rid of his feelings by pounding on a blob of modeling clay, hitting a lot of wooden pegs with a wooden hammer, or kicking some solid piece of furniture. He loved it.

The few times Tommy did start misbehaving, there were no long lectures, accusations, or questions such as "What have I done to deserve a bad boy like this?" Instead, Tommy was made to feel that he was loved and he was not made to feel guilty. There was added inspiration for him to be good because he was made to feel that there were people who wanted to help him to be good. In addition, his mother was able to reach an understanding with him about his feelings of jealousy; she was able to recognize how his viciousness was only the accumulation of his resentment against his baby brother and that there was so much of it that it had to come out somewhere. As time went on, it came out less in the form of hatred and more in the long talks he and his mother had, talks about his jealousy of his younger brother. For the most part, what she said to him consisted of variations of this theme: "I know you are jealous. . . . You think I love him more than I love you, but I don't. . . . When you think he's getting more of anything than you are, let me know. . . . You don't like to have the baby around to take up our time, do you? But don't worry. Daddy and I love you and we will always love you."

The encouraging thing about such an approach to a behavior problem is that it always works. There is something magical about understanding; in addition, understanding is essential as well as effective. Punishment convinces the child that he *is* bad; at the same time it is an emotional release for his parents, who look on his misbehavior as a reminder that they made mistakes as parents.

It's not true that the child whose parents give him everything he needs takes the attitude that he can go in for completely undisciplined behavior. Usually the child who has been given what he needs and doesn't have to fight for it will accept regulations and rules without too much fuss. An unhappy child can go on beating up his classmates every day and still not get rid of his feelings; also, he may be punitive toward his parents because he is unhappy.

Parents have to teach a child that we do not hurt people, or break furniture, or destroy the property of others. How else are children to learn? But if parents want the children to believe them, they must show them that they are going to respect their rights and feelings. The parents' attitude toward the child is the important factor, whether they are giving him food as an infant, or toilet training him, or teaching him the niceties of social behavior.

Throughout this book there are instances of jealousy which show that it is not an isolated problem to be treated with a list of specific instructions. It occurs with other problems which are the result of parental attitudes, and it is best handled by parents' changing their feelings and attitudes.

We are lucky in that we have more chances to change our attitudes; at every stage of growth from infancy to adulthood we can have our emotional lives straightened out for us, or straighten them out ourselves. So, when parents think they have made mistakes and are faced with the prospect of being saddled with a holy terror, they shouldn't give up. They will have another chance, but it means they will probably have to work harder at understanding their child's problems. They can, if necessary, spoil the baby to his heart's content. It will save them a fortune in rods.

CHAPTER V

The First Steps in Handling Jealousy

THIS chapter outlines in a preliminary way some of the things parents ought to know about jealousy; by anticipating it and being prepared for it, they will be better able to cope with it. Here I will outline some of the problems that will be considered in detail in the remaining chapters. However, I must point out that I am not going to give a list of rules to memorize; these are recommendations you can use to reinforce your common sense. Parenthood should be deeply satisfying and enjoyable; mothers and fathers should not feel that studying their children's problems will destroy their spontaneity. The opposite is true: knowing what to expect makes parents more relaxed. If they are ready to accept a child's jealousy as normal they will be able to see that he is lovable too.

First of all, they should be aware that the child may be puzzled by a change—not only when the new baby arrives, but even before that. There are many things about the infant's arrival that he won't understand unless he is prepared for them. Even then he will feel somewhat upset; adults, for example, are able to anticipate separation from one another, but that doesn't ease their sense of loss when it comes. The child is going to be faced with a new and difficult situation after the baby comes, and it is necessary that both he and his parents be prepared for it. For a long time it was felt that if parents told their children of the impending arrival of a baby brother or sister, that was all they had to do. We know now that we prepare the child for the new baby not only to satisfy his sexual curiosity (by telling him where the baby came from), but also to prepare him psychologically for the arrival of someone who may turn out to be a threat to him.

However, statistics show that serious problems with jealousy occur as frequently when the child is told as when he is not told. It isn't that preparing the child in advance is useless, but the failure to follow up the advantage nullifies its effect. It *is* useless to tell him that a baby is coming if you are going to neglect him after the baby arrives. One parent who was disillusioned because of a very serious problem of jealousy in his children told me that he thought it was foolish to tell the child in advance. He said: "With my children it would be a question of forewarned is forearmed. They will just have that much more time to think of new ways to torture the baby." He is a bitter man, and very disappointed that his children aren't better adjusted.

It doesn't require much imagination to understand that children will notice the changes in their mother brought on by her pregnancy. They are puzzled by what they see. They may think that the mother is unattractive, or that she is sick. They know that the other children in the neighborhood make fun of odd people, and they will be terribly hurt if their mother is made to look ridiculous. Then, after she has returned to normal, they will find a direct connection between the way she looked and the arrival of the new baby. They will blame the baby for what happened to the mother, much to the baby's discredit. Starting at the age of two, a child will be able to recognize these differences in his mother's contour, and for this reason it's a good idea to tell children, at that age, what is going on.

Among other things to be considered before the new baby arrives, depending on the age of the older child, is the question of his sleeping arrangements. If he is less than two years old, he should be permitted to stay in his own crib and another crib should be bought for the new baby. If he is old enough to sleep in a bed anyway, he should be allowed to begin sleeping there months before the baby arrives. His promotion to the bed should be attended by some verbal recognition of his new status: he is now big enough to be able to get in and out by himself, to have grown-up size sheets, perhaps even to choose his own bed. With or without the fanfare, the important thing is to impress on him that sleeping in the bed is a reward. He should be told that it's more attractive, and it should be pointed out that he is growing up. He shouldn't have any reason to suspect that he is being given second-best to make room for the baby.

Nursery school for the older child is a good idea if the mother isn't able to cope with him and the baby, but it is important to think of that a long time before the baby is born. If he is sent off to school for the first time *after* the baby arrives, he'll think his mother can't stand him, that she has to get rid of him. He'll resent the baby for getting him out of the house and he won't like the school, either.

The same applies to his being sent to a camp, if he is going for the first time. There is apt to be some trouble if the baby is born in June, because camp starts in July; again, he must not get the idea that he is being exiled because no one has time for him any more. Start talking about camp or school, or a trip to his grandmother's, long before the baby is born. Talk about it before you even tell him about the impending baby. Don't make it sound like an afterthought: "There's going to be a new baby, son. . . . By the way, wouldn't you like to go to camp?" He may not say it, but he will think: "What? And miss all the fun here at home?"

He may want to be there and see the baby being born; it sounds impossible to him that the process can take place as it was described. He has a right to feel curious about it, and, again depending on his age, he will want to relate this to what he knows about sex. If he doesn't know about sex this is a good time for you to tell him, provided you think he can understand what you are talking about.

A simple explanation is best because the child will absorb only a little of the information. Don't think that you have to go into detail—unless he asks—because he will ask questions again and again, as he grows older, each time absorbing a little more according to what he can understand. Clarify things for him. Explain that no one but nurses and doctors can be around when it happens. Try to avoid the impression that the birth process is a sickness, or that there is suffering connected with it: he may resent the baby for what it makes you suffer, and he may even feel guilty for having made you suffer when *he* was born.

When parents tell their child that a baby is on its way, they shouldn't promise him it will be a baby brother or a baby sister, even if he has a preference. He will be upset if they don't make good. Children are imaginative, but they seem to have no imagination: they take the things parents say too seriously. They will amuse themselves by creating all kinds of characters, and they will resent any hints from grownups that their playmates are invisible. Yet when it comes to the words of adults, they will hang on to those words and fling them back at their parents at the first opportunity. They suddenly go literal on one. They don't recognize sarcasm and they miss the subtleties of inflection that adults depend on so much.

If parents tell a child he is going to have a baby *brother* or a baby *sister*, he will make his plans accordingly, and they are adding to the troubles he already has, as well as to the troubles he is going to have, by disappointing him. It would be not too unusual if the child assumed that they were deliberately disappointing him. Parents shouldn't bring up the subject themselves: they shouldn't refer to the forthcoming "baby brother" or "baby sister," but rather to the arrival of "the baby." If the child is too young it will be hard to tell him about the differences between boys and girls; it is better to avoid offering any information at all. Of course, one can't escape when he brings up the subject himself. He'll say, "I'd like to have a baby brother so that when he grows up I can fight with him," or play with him, or let him join the gang, or help him beat up the girls in the neighborhood. Parents shouldn't agree with him that they would like to see a baby boy too, because he will think that they are disappointed when it turns out to be a girl, and their disappointment might give him another reason to dislike her.

A child should be told the truth, that there is no way of knowing, with variations of this theme depending on the ability of the child to understand. You might say, for example, that it's going to be a surprise, to you as well as to him. The boy who is promised a baby brother and gets a baby sister may think that his parents prefer girls to boys. If he is looking forward to a baby sister and finds a baby brother instead, he may feel that he has been inadequate as a male and that his parents are trying again. You can't win. Just don't promise anything. Tell him the truth: you just don't know.

Probably the best way to get the older child interested in the arrival of the new baby is to let him in on the preparations. He should be allowed to help you when you go shopping for the things the baby will need—more than that, ask his advice about some of the things you buy and be sure to follow it if you do ask him. There will be lots of purchases you have to make in advance: sheets, blankets, pads, nightgowns, and so on. You may even need a new bassinette and a carriage, if you have given the older one's away. Nothing will give the child a greater feeling of being a part owner, as it were, of the new baby than co-operation. It will be an introduction to his helping with the baby later, too. But never should he be *forced* to help, either in the preparations or after the baby is born.

A lot has been written on what to do when the baby arrives, but not much about the older child who may be around at the time. The mother who has her baby at home is in danger of creating a very unfortunate impression on the child. If she screams he may feel that something terrible is happening to her. He knows that she is being hurt. It happens at a time when it is impossible to explain anything to him, usually because there is no one around who has time to explain anything. Obviously he will connect his mother's suffering with the appearance of the baby, and he will have more reason to resent the new arrival.

Even when the baby is born in a hospital, the infant's first appearance at home may be upsetting. The mother has returned from the hospital. She is a little disoriented, because there are so many things and people to pay attention to all at once. The father is usually in a dither, and so are the other relatives who came over to welcome the mother home. Even the new baby's nurse is no help. She is preoccupied with the baby and she, too, ignores the older child.

Our hero is left standing on the side lines. He has never been so neglected in his life. This is what comes of separation and of trusting his parents. But it's only the beginning. He doesn't know yet that he can look forward to being awakened at night by the baby's crying, being overlooked when his mother feeds the baby, and playing a very muted second fiddle. Now he will have to learn to walk on tiptoe and he will have to speak in whispers.

The situation is harder for him that first day if he hasn't been prepared for his mother's stay in the hospital. He has probably never before been separated from her for so long a time, and he can't understand her preoccupation with anyone but himself. It is better to avoid an abrupt separation when the time comes to go to the hospital. Arrangements should be made with a nurse, or whoever is going to take care of him, to be around a few weeks or even a month before the mother leaves for the hospital. She herself should start with short absences, so that he will be in less of a panic when she is away for a longer time.

There are other possible arrangements, if the child cannot stay at home. His grandmother, or other relatives whom the child knows and who love him, could invite him to stay with them for a while. A mother shouldn't be upset if a child misses her less and less as time goes on and transfers a lot of affection to his relatives or to the nurse. The more people around whom he likes, the better off he will be.

The father can play a more important role in the child's

life during the hospital stay. There are too many fathers today who never have enough time to play with their children.
But they should make good use of this period. Some fathers
plan their vacations to coincide with the arrival of the baby.
All the children seem to enjoy it: fathers make less fuss about
tidying, hand washing, or early bedtime, so that there is more
time to build a good play city, or swing in the park, or visit
the zoo. Even mealtimes are special events, maybe because
they are not so carefully planned as when the mother is at
home. When the new baby arrives and gets a great deal of
admiration, the father can easily give the older child a genuine sense of his own importance. Babies are enchanting, but
older children also have endearing qualities which are lost if
they are overlooked or neglected.

If the child can be at home with his father, or with a nurse,
or with a housekeeper whom he knows, so much the better.
Even if the mother's homecoming is hectic, the child can help
prepare for it too, by making something with Daddy, buying
flowers for Mother, or helping to tidy his room before she
comes. All this will help make the event a big day and an
exciting reunion. Few mothers are so tired when they return
that they cannot spend some time hugging the older child and
listening to what he says in the first few moments, telling him
how happy she is to be home, how much she missed him, and
only much later asking: "Do you want to see our baby?"

If the child has been away from home and comes back
after mother and infant have returned, he should certainly
not have to walk into a disorganized, preoccupied household
where his mother doesn't have time to greet him and his
father is busy with the new baby. Not only has he not had the
fun of preparing for his mother's return, or experienced the
thrill of seeing her come home, but nobody seems to have
time to welcome him. It's as if he weren't even missed. The
basis for all the preoccupation is a squalling infant, a baby
sister who has the grownups making a highly unnecessary
fuss over her, and, when he looks closely, it's virtually the
same fuss they made over him up to the time he went to

visit his grandmother. What is more, they don't even speak English to her: they gargle in her ear. She is nowhere near as funny as they think she is, but they are suddenly easy to amuse. They laugh at her when she does absolutely nothing and the rest of the time they smile. What in heaven's name has she got that makes them stick their heads into the crib and rub their cheeks against her, pick her up, smell her, hold her, and make love to her? And another thing: she is allowed to be too noisy, and he is forced to be too quiet.

He has to have an explanation for his parents' neglect. They used to make love to him exclusively, and they don't any more. It could be because there is something wrong with him. But it must be a whale of a something if they can make love to someone useless like her, and he must be pretty bad if they prefer the little, if anything, she has. It can only mean that they approve of her, and they don't approve of him. He knows that he had to work like a beaver all his life to hold on to their love and to get their approval. Every time he looked around for his mother he was being neglected; he had to cry to get what he wanted. Even then he worried because he wasn't always sure that she would be there. But the habit of worrying grew and here it is paying off. Now he is *really* worried. The thought occurs to him that they got another baby because he wasn't enough, which means that he wasn't good enough.

Those early weeks after the baby arrives are easily the most important. In the first place, if one doesn't watch out here, all the preparations that have been made will be wasted. He may appear to be more interested in the new baby than in anything else; he probably is, but it can be only on the surface, and most likely because he is expected to register such an interest. Deep down inside him there is one question he wants answered, and he will be looking for the answer day after day and year after year, for as long a time as the other child remains a threat to him: "Am I still loved as much as I ever was?"

Don't be misled into thinking that this curiosity about the

baby, or even his willingness to help take care of her, are proof that he is secure and untroubled. Yes, he loves her, in the same way that he loves his stuffed animals: they are cute and lovable. When he plays with them he is imitating his parents, for which he will get approval; but the stuffed animals also serve as companions, perhaps even as substitutes for the love he needs so much to get from his mother. His toy friends understand him much better than anyone else can, and they can be transformed into anybody at all. They can be grownups or they can be children his age. The new baby has all these advantages, he thinks, and what's more, it moves. So of course he wants to play with the baby, and he may even appear to want to take exclusive charge. But remember, this is the only toy he has ever had which he must share with his parents.

That puzzles him and it may bother him, too, because normally a child isn't interested in sharing. He would rather keep all of his possessions to himself; that has been his right for years. (There are no exceptions to this. Boys don't really like to share their electric trains with their fathers, nor do girls like to share dollhouses with their mothers.) When the child is unsure of his rights, it is only natural that he will begin to distrust those who are depriving him of them. He will begin to take note of their interest in the baby and wonder why it is. He will want the things that she has, and he will resent the care they give her.

I do not want parents to feel that they must neglect the baby, or stop loving her, in order to make the older child feel wanted. This would be artificial and strained and the older child would probably catch on anyway; besides, the infant needs affection too. On the other hand, those too extravagant and overecstatic exclamations about the baby are silly; the older child will probably be hurt by a flow of superlatives about the baby. Besides, it is tactless disregard for his feelings. One wouldn't do it to an adult, so why shouldn't one use good taste with a child too? He has learned that his parents show their love for him in a certain way, with a certain amount of fuss, and he will learn that they love the baby too. But if they exaggerate this love with marked overacting, he can't help but feel that they love her more.

It's natural for him to want to assume possession of the baby and want to help take care of her. He will begin to feel important, especially when the baby starts to recognize him and smile at him. When that happens, he will even want to show her off to the other children in the neighborhood, so he will volunteer to take her out in the carriage. He won't need urging to help take care of her; he'll do it if he wants to, in his own good time, and for the reasons I have mentioned. But he won't go anywhere near her if he feels that she is more important to his parents than he is.

This can be the impression he gets of the baby when parents forget themselves to the extent that the household revolves around her instead of around both of them. The best time to fuss over the baby is when she is being fed. She needs it more then than at any other time, especially if she is a bottle baby and not being breast-fed. Unfortunately the older child is most liable to feel the first and most intense pangs of jealousy when he sees the baby being fed. He will want to watch if he knows that it is going on because he is also very curious about the process. In a primitive society every child has the opportunity to see other mothers nursing their babies quite openly and casually. In our society, it is often a new experience for the child. Even if he has seen kittens or puppies getting food, he will still want to see how a human infant is fed.

It isn't uncommon for him to want to try sucking on the bottle, or on his mother's breast, when he sees her feeding the baby. Let him: it is a very disillusioning experience. Some of the cases described later on in the book were seen at a clinic where it was common practice to have a baby bottle filled with water on the desk. Children who felt at all insecure, and especially those who had a problem with jealousy, would ask if they could suck on the bottle. They were always told to go ahead, because it was a very encouraging sign: it meant that the child knew he could do things in the clinic that he might be criticized for at home. Sometimes this would go on during the first interview and never be repeated, and sometimes one could just about judge how disturbed he was at home by the fact that he would start drinking from the bottle again as later interviews went on.

It is not necessarily a sign of hopeless insecurity in the child if he wants to do that when he watches his mother nursing the baby, nor does it have to be jealousy that prompts him. The normal, mentally healthy child may never have had enough nursing, and he is subconsciously reminded of the pleasure it gave him a long time ago. One really can't blame him for wanting to try it again and above all he shouldn't be thwarted when he asks to do it. That will only convince him—as he already suspects—that the newcomer has advantages and privileges that he can't have.

All children, no matter how much love, understanding, and security their parents have given them, will feel a certain amount of jealousy of the baby. At the same time, because the baby is helpless and doll-like, and because his parents will give him approval if he is nice to her, he really loves her, too. Ideally, the approach should be to play down whatever might make him jealous and leave him only with love for her. It's a nice idea, but it rarely works. It's impractical because his jealousy is there, whether it's hidden or on the surface, and it's up to you to recognize it and to avoid making it more of a problem than it has to be.

There are a whole lot of remarks tending to overemphasize the importance of the baby which should be avoided. Among them are variations of "Shh-h! You'll wake the baby!" "Why do you have to come in here to play?" "Don't do that, she'll catch cold." He'll learn soon enough that if he wakes the baby he's the one who will suffer: he will get less attention than when the baby is asleep. Also, if he finds out that the baby's sleep is important to you, he will have a weapon to use to get revenge, when it occurs to him to get revenge. One bad feature of such remarks is their emphasis on the change that has to take place in his life, which he thinks is entirely unwarranted. It has taken him a long time to get used to the uncertainties that normally occur in even the best-regulated families, and he will resent anything that will curb his hard-earned freedom. Frequently it reaches the point where even things that are meant to give him pleasure are devices, he firmly believes, to get rid of him so that his parents can pay more attention to the baby. That's why sending him to nursery school after the baby is born may arouse in him a great dislike for school. And in the same way, he may go off to camp convinced that, with all of its pleasurable advantages, camp is partly something that was thought up to get him out of the way and give the baby a clear field.

The child is suspicious of his parents and their motives and it will need some very careful explaining on their part every time they want him to make less noise and not wake the baby. They have to go into great detail and remind him over and over again that the baby is helpless, that sometimes she is a nuisance, that she does take up a lot of his mother's time, and that these are a few of the disadvantages of having a baby. It will encourage him to be told that she will eventually grow up and be much less trouble; most encouraging of all is to have this drilled into him over and over again: "Mother loves you, and she doesn't love you less because the baby is here."

If his father has not been in the habit of calling up two or three times a day, it is something he should avoid doing after the baby is born, unless it can be done when the older child is away from the house. He will suspect that Dad's interest in the baby is greater than his interest in him, especially if he doesn't remember his father ever calling up just to ask how *he* was. For another thing, Dad's first remarks on coming home should be addressed to the older child, exactly the same as before the baby was born. Despite his impatience to rush in and see how the baby is getting along, he should greet the older child first and say "How are you?" and joke with him or whatever it was he always did or said, and in exactly the same way. After a decent interval, depending on how long he can contain himself, or when the older child becomes diverted by something else, he can pay his respects to the infant.

Fathers have to learn to curb their impatience, and both fathers and mothers would do well to curb their relatives' enthusiasm. The most harm is done by well-meaning friends and relatives, who may make the mistake of saying "I came to see the baby." It's bad enough when it's the first baby in the family, because it implies a lack of interest in the baby's parents, who may be sensitive people. However, they are nowhere near as sensitive as the older child who rushes out to greet the guests, only to find that they are no longer interested in him, and, in fact, have been spending their time purchasing valuable gifts for the baby. He retires, disappointed, to his room, if he is the type that broods; or he will burst into the baby's room, where the sycophants are busy admiring the infant, and yell, "Hey, look at me! Look at my engine! Look at me recite! Look at me dance! Hey, for Pete's sake, won't somebody *please* look at me?"

When you buy a layette, make a note to include, as every outfit for an expected second child should include, a large assortment of gifts appropriate for the older one, to be given him from time to time, or as frequently as relatives will come around with a gift for the baby and none for her brother. It's usually something she can wear, or chew on, or make a noise with. The idea is that it's useful and more to be appreciated by her parents than by the baby, who is much too young to do very much appreciating anyway. Therefore, it's important that the gift for the older child should not be clothing, but a toy or a game of some sort; it should be something that *he* can appreciate; also, he should be able to tell himself that it's better than what the baby got and related directly to his interests and abilities.

Some parents and relatives err in assuming an equality between the infant and the older child that is not real. For example, Georgiana, whom I spoke about in Chapter I, was given exact duplicates of whatever toys her baby brother received. Though she was only a year older than the baby, she had different capacities and interests and it would have been much wiser to recognize them. Her greater maturity was hard won and it did not help to belittle her independence by making her only the equal of an infant.

One thing that always seems to happen when people are around is that the mother is asked questions about, and falls into the trap of comparing, the obstetrical difficulties in the births of the two children. One should never make this remark, or anything which sounds like it: "I had a much easier time with this one." If the older child happens to overhear such a statement—and he probably will—he won't forget it in a hurry.

Avoid making comparisons between the children, at any cost and at any age. When they are older, both of them are liable to suffer. I am coming back to this a little later. When the baby is still new, the older one may ask questions which call for comparing him with the infant. These can be harmless, and really informative; they may be an occasion for an absorbing story. For example, when he watches his mother nurse the baby, she can say something like this: "You were once as little as she is, and you had to be fed this way, too." This is an interesting idea to him and, in fact, can be made a very important selling point when she is trying to get him interested in the baby. As time goes on, he will be interested in all the changes that take place, and he will want to have explanations as well as comparisons.

Parents can be truthful, but they do have a poetic license to dramatize his infancy. If he asks: "Did I cry as much as the baby?" this is a possible answer: "You didn't have a chance to cry very much because Daddy and I were so worried about you that we *rushed* to your room whenever we heard a noise. We looked for pins and we said 'Do you suppose he has a tummy-ache?' But you did cry loudly when you cried; we thought you had the *loudest* cry we had ever heard. Everybody said you must be a strong baby. I guess you just wanted something to eat in a hurry."

"Did I ever wear diapers?"

"Yes, you did. As a matter of fact, the diaper-service man would say to me: 'Are you *sure* you have only one baby? I think he must be very big, because I deliver *so* many diapers to you!' Then he'd go away shaking his head, wondering what we did with all those diapers."

And so on. If parents have ever tried this sort of intimate biography, they will know how effective it is. I have seen eight-year-olds so absorbed that they won't let parents stop telling them stories about themselves, even though they know it is partly made up. Feeding time for the baby can be story time for his brother. He will laugh and chuckle because he was so big, or so little, or such a noise-maker, or such a sound sleeper. The mother can keep lolly-pops in a convenient place in her room, or an assortment of toys he can tinker with as she feeds the baby. Or let it be the time when he has an ice-cream cone, so that he has the oral satisfaction of eating while the baby is being fed. (Forget about the taboo against eating between meals; that isn't nearly so important.) A young child is never so interested as when a story concerns himself, and, being human, he likes it dramatized.

But parents *do* have to be honest about their feelings, otherwise their child may collect data about sex and babies, but remain confused about the emotions which make them worth while. The parents *do* love the baby, and they *don't* feel that she is nasty because she needs to be diapered, or fed. They love the older child, too; they recognize what he can do now, but they are not ashamed of his babyhood or anything connected with it.

Therefore, it isn't wise to disparage or ridicule the baby's lack of toilet training, or to compliment the older child by telling him that he is better than the baby because he has learned to control himself. If he is worried about the attention that the baby is getting, and impressed by the fact that she gets a good deal more attention when her diapers have to be changed, he may suddenly return to bed wetting and forget his toilet training. This could be resentment of his parents for not paying more attention to him, or it could be that he has figured out that this is the way to get more attention, inasmuch as it works pretty successfully with the baby. He will feel guilty and ashamed of himself because he has done something his mother just got through telling him is something babies do because they don't know any better, and not what grown-up boys would do. The child who becomes a bed wetter under such circumstances should be treated for jealousy, and not for bed wetting, and the treatment of his jealousy will be much easier if he isn't ashamed and anxious about something else.

At about this time, when the older child is helping with the baby, he will begin to notice the physical differences between boys and girls. Children's ideas on the subject seem to be very firmly entrenched; even when things are explained as carefully as possible, they will hold on to their original impressions. Apparently a difference in the human body itself is too much for a child to understand: a penis is like an arm or a leg and the lack of it would be painful and crippling. If he were to lose any part of his body so painfully it could only happen as punishment for being bad, or if someone didn't like him and decided to tear it off. A child who sees a one-legged man senses the difficulties he has in getting around, and he firmly hopes that nothing like that will happen to him. He can't understand that his baby sister was born without a penis. All he knows is that she doesn't have one right now. But she must have had one once and lost it; he thinks that she is going to be inconvenienced because she won't be able to urinate. He is filled with fear that he will lose his own, and his anxiety about the possibility of such a loss becomes intensified whenever he thinks he has been bad.

The older girl who sees her baby brother's penis for the first time may first be filled with envy that she doesn't have one and then may conclude that she must have been born with one but that it was taken away (or that she lost it) because she was bad. This subject has to be explained to children very carefully and in the most simple language, not once, but over and over again, whenever mothers sense that their children are troubled by it. The girl who is jealous because of the advantages her younger brother seems to have will tie it all in with the fact that he has a penis and she doesn't have one. She may feel cheated; as time goes on she will become more and more envious of the privileges and advantages that men have, so that she may become extremely competitive with men.

As the children grow older, the problem of their jealousy becomes harder to handle. The mother is now required to develop more physical agility than she ever had before. It's a question of almost constant watching, of planning on not ounces, but pounds, of prevention. She must be speedier than the children; to prevent their injuring each other, she must know in advance when a blow is to be struck and prevent it from reaching its goal. Punishing the child after he has hit the other one will make him feel worse about what he has done. And she shouldn't try to appeal to his sportsmanship: telling him that he shouldn't hit the baby because she is so small and helpless is useless. Her being smaller and helpless has convinced him that she has the advantage over him. These are the very things which make his parents fonder of her and have caused him to be jealous. What the mother would be saying, in effect, would be, "Don't hit the baby because she deserves to be hit and because you want to hit her."

Therefore, when the child is older, the mother has to plan her time a little more carefully, especially when she bathes or feeds the infant. The father can help out here by playing with the older one, or one may have to get extra help at that time of the day. Or perhaps, after the baby is fed and put to bed, one can plan something special for the older child. He might be allowed to have dinner with you each night, or there could be a long reading period as a tribute to his maturity and interest. Even with an only child the evening hour is hard; the mother and the child are both tired and out of patience. The child may take out his crankiness on the baby and the mother's impatience will be shown by displeasure and scolding. Tired mothers, tired children, and jealousy too often add up to loss of temper and tears. It is therefore wise to anticipate these low spots in the day and to try harder than ever to be at your most understanding and most forgiving.

A child should know that he is entitled to feel any way he wants to about his brother or sister, and he is not to think that he is a bad child because of it. He will be less worried if he knows that he can express himself honestly and if he can talk about his dislikes, but he must be allowed to do it without his parents making him feel hateful because he hates. It must have occurred to parents by this time that a child is not really a monster just because he doesn't love his sister; parents have to be very sure they don't think so in order not to give him the idea that he is one. He will feel bad when he hurts the other child and he will be convinced of his wickedness if he is punished. Again parents must remember that he is too young to be able to control his temper, and he needs someone to check his impulse, someone who can grab the clenched fist, the open palm, or the thrown missile. He would like to follow through at the moment, but he will be much more grateful for restraint, when he is restrained from being bad.

Parents don't end the destructive desire by stopping him from inflicting damage; the impulse is still there and so is his anger. He should be distracted immediately. Get him interested in some other toys in another part of the room, or, if at all possible, in another part of the house. Parents should prepare themselves in advance for this, and try to think up all sorts of things for him to do. Their watchfulness should be directed toward protecting the baby without ever giving the older child the idea that he isn't loved.

When both children are old enough to make friends outside the home, they should not be encouraged to have the same friends. This makes it seem that the older child has to take care of the younger one; also, the younger child is at a disadvantage when he fails in competition with older children. They shouldn't be urged to share their possessions with each other; they may be too young to have so noble an impulse as generosity. Their natural impulse is to be selfish, to hold on to their own possessions, because they may have grown up to feel insecure about the love their mother was supposed to give them. When a child finds something tangible to hold on to, like a toy, don't expect him to give it up. It's natural that he should hold on to it, and it's a sign that he is growing more intelligent: he can recognize differences in the values of things.

Comparing the two children when they are older, or giving one an advantage over the other, can do more than anything else to create in them a dislike for each other and destroy any feeling of love and understanding. When a mother says to her son, "Why can't you be nice and quiet like your little sister?" a whole series of reactions sets in which tends to make him worse, instead of better. His mother's statement means that she disapproves of him because he isn't nice and quiet enough; if she disapproves, that means that he is bad. The model of niceness and quietness is his younger sister, who is getting the approval that he should have had. He is jealous that his sister gets more approval than he, he resents his mother for not giving him enough approval, and he makes no effort to try to be nice and quiet because it's hopeless: he can't be nice and quiet because he is a bad boy. Children resign themselves to being inferior to their brothers and sisters when they have been given enough proof, all their lives, that their brothers or sisters are getting more love and more approval than they.

There is one thing that children demand and will always resent not having: fair and equal treatment. One of the disadvantages of punishing one child for striking the other is that you have no way of knowing that he may have been provoked into striking the blow. He thinks that he was justified and sometimes he is, especially if the other child has tormented him and goaded him, on purpose, just to get him in trouble. (This is sneaky behavior; he does it, perhaps, because he thinks the other one is getting more love.) The child who was punished is impressed with the injustice of the punishment, and he feels martyred in addition to feeling that he is a bad child. There are people whom we call defensive, who are always explaining their motives and defending their actions, who are always ready with alibis and excuses. They seem to expect punishment and are trying to ward it off. Much of this stems from parents' lack of fair play, as when they have punished a child when he was innocent, even though it may have been the first time in months that he was innocent.

One of the best ways in the world for parents to create jealousy in their children is to reward the one who helps them and not the other. The one who gets rewards for doing the dishes, making the beds, doing homework promptly, and so on, is the child her mother takes as a model, to compare her with her less co-operative brother. There is a temptation for the younger one to behave so that she will win rewards, and not necessarily out of a healthy spirit of co-operation. The older child will sense this more quickly than his parents; he will be resentful and determined not to help at all. He knows the real motive behind his sister's attempts to ingratiate herself, that she is trying to do him out of his parents' affections; he is hurt because his parents can't see through her and because they continue to think that she is a paragon.

The older the children are, the more they will be impressed by the advantages one has that the other doesn't have, and by the fact that their parents may be playing favorites. Sometimes the parents just can't seem to avoid making one child the favorite, because there is usually the temptation to compare the two. It requires a change of attitude in parents. It isn't as if the two children were part of a team, one member of which is good and the other bad. Each child is an individual and has to be treated as one; each child has problems which are important to him. These problems don't have to be handled in relation to the problems of the other children. If parents could convince themselves that each child in the family is a separate unit, they would have far less trouble with jealousy in their children.

I have a friend who has a very remarkable understanding of the problems of jealous children; he openly admits that it is the result of his psychoanalysis. He is better liked by children of all ages than any other person I ever met, and he is the terror of their parents. I have seen him go about his cam-

paign, which he insists is helpful to the children and not necessarily an attempt to get himself universally loved. (He thinks
that that is only a by-product because he is on their side.) Once
the two of us were week-end guests of some friends whose two
daughters were aged seventeen and fourteen. Evelyn, the
seventeen-year-old, was traveling through Europe on a tour
with other girls in her high-school graduating class. Jane was
an attractive though bitter member of the second-year class in
high school and shared Evelyn's room, which was plastered
from floor to ceiling with pictures of Evelyn's exploits. Her
parents told my friend a number of times that it was too bad
he had never met Evelyn: "There's a girl for you!" My friend
rose to the situation immediately.

After the third or fourth time they regretted Evelyn's ab-
sence, he turned to Jane and said, just loud enough so that
her parents couldn't hear, "That Evelyn sounds pretty insuffer-
able to me." Jane was startled and looked at him to see if he
was serious. She was loyal and only partially grateful.

"She is very beautiful," Jane said. "Everybody likes her."

"I don't see how," said my friend. "It seems to me that anybody who is so perfect would be pretty tough to live with."

Jane smiled and you could see that she was warming to him.
He continued, "She must be very conceited, to plaster her face
all over her bedroom. She probably makes a big act of being
modest. I have seen the type. They go to college and join the
best sororities, but they lead very unhappy lives after they get
married because they can't win any more prizes. I'll bet you a
hundred dollars that she doesn't take those pictures along with
her after she's married."

By this time Jane was laughing. "It's kid stuff," she said,
"isn't it?"

"You can bet your life it is," he said. "It's kid stuff, and it's
for people who take a long time to grow up."

Jane's loyalty dissolved. "She is conceited, you know, and
she puts on a terrific act about being modest. If her friends
only knew the way she really felt about them . . ."

"That's what I mean," he said. "They're insincere, and I think that you hardly ever find sincerity in politicians."

"That's what she is, a politician," Jane said. "Anybody can do what she does if they want to be insincere."

"Poor but honest, Jane," he said, "that's us, poor but honest. We'll go through life painting our bedroom walls a neutral color and ten dollars gets you a thousand dollars that we're much nicer people and we'll be happier in the long run."

Jane followed him around for the rest of the week end, and he rarely missed an opportunity to belittle Evelyn in absentia and praise Jane. All he was doing was to capitalize on Jane's resentment of her older sister. She was so relieved that she was able to express it and to have some help in saying it that she was suddenly more pleasant, less bitter, and noticeably happier.

When we drove back to the city my friend said, "You know, if Evelyn is superior to Jane she must be a sort of female Superman." I knew Evelyn pretty well, and I knew that his next remark was true: "Evelyn was probably jealous of Jane when Jane was born," he said. "I wouldn't be a bit surprised if her need to go out after all kinds of awards and be elected the most likely to succeed is the direct result of that."

On another occasion I witnessed his approach to a boy of nine whose sister was three years younger. Their parents were very proud that the girl was able to sing and they practiced songs with her, hopeful that she might become a musician someday. One afternoon they called on her to give us a recital and the nine-year-old boy sat politely in his chair to listen. My friend sat down alongside of him, applauded moderately when his sister finished her song, then turned to him and said, "I hate music. Don't tell this to anyone, but what I hate most about music is girls singing. Is there any place we can go to get away from this?"

The boy burst into laughter, and he and my friend went on a tour of the house.

This is a radical and a highly unorthodox approach to the problem of jealousy. My friend feels that he has to do it because parents obviously don't. He becomes acutely upset when mothers mention the Evelyns and neglect the Janes, when they call on the geniuses of the family to perform and make an audience of the non-artists. He feels that he is giving first aid, and he really believes that it is beneficial. He says he serves as a sort of valve through which most of the resentment is released, leaving less resentment behind.

"At least," he says, "they know that they have someone on their side who seems to think that they're the more important ones. Now how many parents do you think can get away with that? They can tell the kids over and over again that they know they're jealous, that they have a right to dislike each other, and it will help some. But how about the kid who can see for himself that his brother is more popular, or that his sister is better than he is? He's got a tough job even to give up the struggle gracefully. They need me, those kids. I'm the guy who tells them they're better. Parents can't do it because they'll have the other ones down on them and then I'd have to play up to *them*."

His own particular trouble, he once told me, was based on a mistake his parents made when he was young. He was seven when his sister was born, and he was made to take care of her. He had to sit with her, to take her around in the carriage, and to suffer the insults of the other members of his baseball and football teams. His resentment of her was not permitted to come out then, but years later he showed a good bit of hostility against women; his callous treatment of them had a very serious effect on his business and social life. That was why he went to be analyzed.

My friend's approach to the problem of jealousy may have worked for a while, but it wasn't honest or mentally healthy. The Janes of this world have to find their satisfactions in themselves and in living comfortably with others, not in belittling people. We don't use others as steppingstones to our own maturity; by respecting them, we respect and develop our own potentialities, too. Jane did not have to make someone else appear ridiculous in order to justify her own worth;

she probably would have made herself decidedly unpopular if she tried it later on with her classmates, or co-workers, or in her social life. Jane may have enjoyed the flattery of my friend who was her parents' contemporary, but she probably felt guilty about disloyalty to her sister and her parents. It was not an honest approach to her problem, for, while her resentment had a chance for expression, there was no sound, constructive attitude to take its place.

Again I feel I have to bring in a comparison between psychiatry and the other branches of medicine, and again to emphasize the importance of prevention of disease. The prevention of some physical disease can be extremely expensive; some prevention programs are world-wide in their scope. Apparently enough people think that it's worth that much money to keep people from suffering from chronic ailments or catching diseases. Prevention of epidemics means that health departments must always be vigilant; they mustn't stop preventing diseases, even for a minute. It's no easier when one is trying to prevent psychological disturbances such as jealousy: it's a job which requires that you be familiar with its first signs and the symptoms, but especially with the causes. When it gets out of hand, don't be afraid to ask for professional advice; but remember that the problem is much more easily solved if it is attended to early.

CHAPTER VI

Jealousy in an Only Child

IN THIS chapter and those following I use typical case histories to show what can happen in certain situations. Some parents whom I have never met or had any contact with may find a resemblance to similar situations in their own families, because these are typical people and real situations.

First we should examine the occurrence of jealousy in a child who has no brothers or sisters: the only child. The only child isn't immune from jealousy just because he has no brothers and sisters; he may be jealous of his father, or the girl only child may be jealous of her mother. Jealousy can complicate the already rather difficult situation in which all only children find themselves. However, it isn't true that the only child has to be a maladjusted child. It's true that he has a couple of strikes on him before he starts: he has to find companionship outside of his family, for instance, and he stays by himself more than do other children. On the other hand, the only child learns to be more independent and self-reliant, even if it's only because he has to compensate for the companionship that he lacks. There are other compensations: the parents of an only child spend so much time with him, including the time they don't have to spend on other children, that their interests are concentrated on his growing up. They teach him more and help to educate him, with the result that the vast majority of only children are more intelligent, as a group, than children from larger families. Unfortunately, these advantages are slight and disappear completely if the parents lack understanding of the potential dangers that lie ahead of their child. By far the worst thing that can happen to an only child, and the easiest, is to have an overprotective mother.

The overprotected child is one who is forced to be dependent after he has just about made up his mind that it's no use being dependent: after all, he was never as dependent as he wanted to be during infancy. It's only natural that he would like to try independence. But all of us go through a stage where we learn that we can no longer be as dependent as we would like to be. One reason some people are immature is that they can't reach independence because they have been frustrated by an overprotective mother.

The mother of an only child is more likely to be overprotective than a mother who has two or more children. For one thing there are no distractions for her: she doesn't have to care for or love more than one child, and concentrates on the one she has. There are dozens of other reasons, too. The only child may have been sickly in infancy; he may have been born after the parents have failed a number of times to have a child; he may have been unwanted, and so on. (Even an unwanted child may be overprotected, because the mother feels guilty and tries to make it up to him.) Then, too, the unconscious factors which make a mother have one child and no more might tend to make her much too interested in her only child.

Let's look at this: a mother may have an abnormal desire to have a son, because of the trouble she has adjusting to married life. A son would seem to her to be a substitute for a husband. There are many such women and there are as a result more only sons than only daughters. Such a mother will not have another child if her first-born is a boy; if her first is a girl she may try again, until she does have a son. Some mothers draw away from their husbands after the son is born, and some use very elaborate, although they may be unconscious, excuses to avoid having more children. The mother of a boy only child may even develop enough physical complaints to avoid another pregnancy. On the other hand there are those women who want a daughter and no other children for other

—and perhaps equally neurotic—reasons. Of course, in this whole discussion of only children, we must not forget that there are mothers who are forced to be satisfied with only one child, either because they were so old at the time the child was born that they can have no more children, or because there are real, not psychological, physical ailments which make child-bearing impossible for them. Nevertheless, in many cases where a girl is the only child, the mother may have been prevented from having more children because of medical reasons; where the boy is the only child, the reasons may be mostly psychiatric.

There's a process called "identification" through which a child learns a pattern of behavior from imitating (identifying with) someone he likes or admires. It can be his parents, an older boy, or girl, a hero in the movies or the comic strips, or anybody. A girl learns femininity by identifying with her mother, while a boy learns masculinity by identifying with his father. In large families the younger children don't always identify with their parents: they are diverted by the older ones, or by friends. Only children can develop greater independence than their age-mates because, not seeing how other children do things day after day, they strive to be like the adults closest to them, their fathers or mothers.

In a family where an only boy has no father, either because of divorce or because of separation, he will be at a loss without a standard of masculine behavior to guide him. Or, even if his father is there, but his mother is overprotective, the father's position may be so unimportant that the child cannot identify with him. The mother continues to be all-important, the father being only a threat to the child's security, so the boy may identify with his mother. This could end up with his taking on some of the feminine characteristics of his mother; when that happens, it can be the start of the kind of maladjustment we call homosexuality. Or, if he doesn't identify with her so completely, he can be exceedingly jealous of his father.

Jealousy in an only child is usually directed toward one or the other of the parents; when he is jealous of other children he may envy their having what he thinks are nicer parents, but

mostly he thinks of their brothers and sisters, who are convenient playmates. For the only child is lonely, and the overprotec-
tion of the mother doesn't quite make up for his need for
companionship. The Oedipus situation can be most obvious
in the only child. The mother who lavishes too much affection
on her son because he is compensation for her unhappiness in
life will be quite content to see him by her side the rest of
her days; she usually tries to discourage him from breaking
away from her. But any overprotective mother who hopes to
gain her child's love in this way may arouse in him an unconscious hatred of her for saddling him with a debt he can never
repay.

I don't want to worry already worried parents too much.
The mention of the Oedipus complex sometimes arouses unnecessary fear. The Oedipus complex concerns the normal attachment of a child to a parent of the opposite sex. Because
the mother is usually responsible for the care of an infant, she
becomes the psychological center, too. It is only when a child
is about six or seven that he begins to appreciate his father.
Yet there are too many mothers who are frightened of every
gesture of love they receive from a son; also, they have heard
so much about "mama's boys" that they don't dare admit even
a little physical love for their children.

Sometimes a little boy will tell his mother he'd like to marry
her someday. All he means is: "At this moment I am secure
and happy, and I love you. I cannot imagine the future without you, because it would mean loneliness and loss of all the
good things I enjoy." It is a perfectly natural expression of his
needs at that age. If, when he is fifteen, she tells him that he
wanted to marry her when he was six, he will be overwhelmed
with embarrassment, or he may not believe her. He will grow
up and away from his mother, but she shouldn't deter him.
And she shouldn't be a sacrificing mother who expects return
for her love. Her dividends will come in seeing a normal,
healthy, happy adolescent who will not have to enter adulthood feeling trapped by what she says she has done for him,
or feeling that he can never repay his debt to her.

The boy who suffers most is the one whose mother refuses to let go of him in time and allows her jealousy of his growing up to interfere with his life. She is jealous of his girl friends, jealous of his regard for his father and his friends; she is too concerned about his trips away from home and gets hysterical when he stays out late. He may resent this in her; marriage for such a person could be an escape from his mother's influence. On the other hand, he could be so strongly tied up in the silver cord she should have cut years before that he may not get married; he prefers to be overprotected because he has been taught to be afraid of independence. If he does marry, it is to someone who promises to be a mother to him in the sense that she will let him be dependent on her. Getting married to escape from a mother's influence, or to continue to be influenced by a mother, are not good enough reasons for getting married.

The case of Louis Maddox is a good example of a child whose mother was overprotective because of her own anxiety and insecurity. When Louis was a baby, she was sure that every symptom he showed meant that he was going to die from a very serious illness. It started with the first time he was sick, when he was three; she thought that he might die and that she would be deprived of his love for the rest of her life, so she spent sleepless nights holding him in her arms and lost a lot of weight.

Louis was in a peculiar position, wanting the love of both of his parents and wanting to love them too. A child needs a father as well as a mother. But he already felt hatred for his father; he was jealous of him and disliked him, because his father took up some of his mother's time; he loved his mother and he wanted her to himself.

It doesn't take a child long to find out the best ways to get the approval of his parents; at the top of the list is this: "Be a good boy; do what your mother tells you to do and Mother will love you." Mrs. Maddox was still upset about her son's early sicknesses and was sure that eating a lot would make Louis very healthy. Louis, in order to get his mother to love him, did what she told him to do: he ate. He ate, too, as an indication of his own uncertainty and need for affection, because he felt uncertain about his mother's love for him. He did what she told him to do, but apparently she loved his father, too; he began to have doubts about how much she *really* loved him, and he began to hate his father.

Meanwhile he continued to eat. It was a sort of desperate attempt to hold on to his mother by devouring everything in sight, just to win her approval. He weighed 140 pounds when he was seven; he was too big for the seats in the second grade in school, but he wasn't ready to go on to the higher grades. He was uncomfortable physically and unhappy mentally because he had to suffer the insults that are aimed at all fat children. And, like all fat children, he was jolly and happy.

That should read: "Like all fat children he *appeared* to be jolly and happy." He wasn't happy, really; he was ashamed of his bigness, his slowness, and his inability to play ball with the other kids, or run, or join them in any sports or games. When they chose sides for a soft-ball game he was the umpire; when they played football he was the center—and everybody piled on Louis because he was such a good sport about it, because he was so fat that he couldn't get hurt, and just because he was fat.

As an only child Louis didn't have to be fat. It is only that his way of winning his mother's approval was to eat, just as she had told him to. Also, he was unsure of her love for him, he was jealous of his father, and he disliked himself because he hated his father. His getting fat was the result of being an only child in the Maddox family. Had he been born an only Jones child he might have grown up differently; as an only Smith child he could have developed a tic; as an only Brown child he could have been bookish and withdrawn. It wasn't that he was an only child that made him the way he was; it was being an only child who hit upon eating as a means of getting approval and, at the same time, satisfied his inner hunger for love by putting things into his belly.

The Maddox family doctor looked Louis over and suggested

a diet. Mrs. Maddox had to be convinced first that her son needed to be thin and that was a job in itself.

"But it's glandular," she told the doctor. "Why can't you give him some pills?"

"It's not glandular," the doctor said. "He's eating too much, that's all."

"But he's always hungry," she said. "I can't let him feel starved."

"Then take him to a psychiatrist," the doctor said. "There's no reason for a seven-year-old boy to be as hungry as he is unless it's mental."

After she got over her shock Mrs. Maddox gave in; Louis went to a psychiatrist with her. She was told that she herself would have to see the psychiatrist, too, because it's easier to handle a child's problems if they aren't complicated by those of the mother. She still didn't like the idea.

"You know," she said, "I still think it's glandular, his being fat. He's been on a diet for a month—the diet our own doctor gave me—and he's still putting on weight."

"Perhaps he's eating food away from home," the psychiatrist said.

"Oh, no," Mrs. Maddox said. "He couldn't be. Where would he get the money? . . . Oh, dear! Now I know!"

"What is it?" he asked.

"I've been missing change from my purse for some time. Maybe he's been buying things to eat on the outside . . . See? He's hungry, poor soul; he's so hungry that he's been driven to stealing. . . . I *know* it's glandular."

In interviews with Louis the doctor learned that Louis stole the money to buy ice cream and candy not only for himself but for the other children, too. He was so desperately in need of friends that he felt he had to bribe them to like him!

Now, this happens from time to time with children in larger families, too, and isn't exclusively the problem of the only child, just as being fat can happen to other than only children. However, too many times the reason is the same: the child is jealous and feels left out of things; he thinks he can't be loved; he feels he has to buy his way into friendships, so he steals. It isn't a sign of criminality; it's proof of loneliness.

Louis, the doctor found out, was filled with feelings of unworthiness and guilt, not only because he stole money, but also because he was mixed up in his feelings. He hated his father, for one thing, and he hated himself because of it. The doctor encouraged him to talk more about his feelings and found that deep down Louis hated his mother, too. Louis didn't want to admit this, even to himself. Outwardly he loved her and he needed her love so much. If she knew he hated her she would never love him, and he wouldn't even let himself think of his hatred.

What made him hate her? Well, for one thing he resented her depriving him of his father's friendship. Unconsciously he was aware that she was keeping him from his father by encouraging him to stay closer to her. This came out only after many, many interviews with the doctor, as did this conversation one day:

"She calls me Sweetheart and Honey and I think she means it, but she doesn't," Louis told the doctor.

"Why do you think she doesn't?"

"I *know* she doesn't, that's why," Louis said.

"Is it because she calls your dad that, too?" the doctor asked.

"I don't know. . . . I guess so."

The situation was explained to Louis and later to his mother. Louis was told about being jealous of his father, and the doctor explained that he didn't have to feel guilty just because he was jealous. His mother learned that she didn't have to feel insulted just because Louis hated her from time to time.

"The only way you can relieve his feelings of guilt," the doctor said, "is by letting him hate or be jealous and by showing him you still love him. Also, how about my seeing Mr. Maddox soon, so that we can find out why he can't start being a father to the boy?"

Louis was sent to a small camp that summer, because it was felt that the gibes of a smaller group could be controlled more easily than those of a large group. The insults a fat boy gets from his friends sometimes make him defensive; he tries to prove that fatness is a virtue and he eats even more. The other boys were told not to poke fun at Louis and the nickname Tiny, which was pinned on him the first day, was dropped in favor of Looey.

His father was encouraged to see him frequently and to do things with Louis which Mr. Maddox was interested in and enjoyed doing, whether it was swimming, tennis, or playing card games. In the course of the summer a better relationship was established between Louis and his father. Mr. Maddox began to feel like a parent for the first time. Also for the first time, Louis was beginning to relax, not only with strangers and boys his own age, but with his father, too; and he began to eat less and he lost weight.

It wasn't just Mr. Maddox's interest in his son that relaxed the boy; it was that Louis was beginning to understand that his jealousy of his father was, in a sense, normal, and that he didn't have to hate himself for his feelings. By getting Louis to understand that he was *permitted* to be jealous, it was possible to relieve some of his anxiety about himself. He became less tense and he was no longer as hungry as he used to be. Those hunger pangs were due to anxiety and nothing else; they weren't glandular, as both the family physician and the psychiatrist knew.

Louis was also helped by the change in Mrs. Maddox. Her own anxiety about protecting Louis was catching; she had passed it on to him and it helped increase his own tension. She found other interests: she joined several clubs, spent more time with her friends, and began to lead a fuller social life than she had before. It wasn't an easy time for her, by any means, but she could see that Louis was happier. When camp was over she encouraged Louis to have his new friends around the house to visit; she even took them all on trips and outings. Her pride in his improvement more than compensated her for the fact that he was growing up.

Only children are not all destined for unhappiness. The very closeness of the group should be a reason for happiness and many of these children grow up excellently adjusted. The smaller family group consists of three people who have a better chance to help each other and understand each other; father, mother, and child are able to share experiences that might be too expensive for larger families. Parents who don't feel hampered by one child will keep on doing things that interest them, things that they enjoy doing. The result has to be beneficial to themselves and to the child. When parents have fun the child is bound to share it, whether they take him to concerts with them, or on camping trips, or sailing, or even for a walk.

Parents of only children need to remember this: here is a situation where children can really be spoiled, not by too much love, but by too much anxiety and abnormal protectiveness. When that happens you will see the overdemanding child who is spoiled for want of a chance to grow up.

The only child needs younger people than his parents; he should be allowed to have other children around, and to create some mess; one needs to learn what children are like, not just *one* child by himself, but in a group. They're noisy and careless; they fight and argue continually—and they have a very good time! It's good for a child to have the feeling of someone or something depending on him: that's why giving him a pet is helpful to his growing up.

His father should plan to spend time with the child. They may even set up a workshop or a playroom where they can be together. The father will find no more appreciative or worthwhile audience than his son, any time he wants to show off what may be his meager baseball technique, or engineering skill. If the child is too young for these things, he can still enjoy his father's company when he plays with his blocks, or goes on walks or on trips to see boats, trains, and planes. Little gifts from the father need not be expensive as long as they fit the child's interests and show that his father knows what boys like.

A child needs to see a pattern of married life that includes affection between his parents. But he shouldn't be shut out: when his father comes home in the evening and kisses his

mother fondly, the father ought to have a hug and a kiss for
Junior, too. There is no reason to hide love, though parents
shouldn't indulge in passionate embraces in front of the child.
That's too private; it makes him feel uncomfortable and uneasy, just as another adult would be embarrassed by any demonstration of highly emotional love-making. A child sees enough
highly charged love in the movies, but he can't get too much
of the kind of real affection and tenderness that should be a
part of marriage. When he does, it gives him the secure feeling that comes only from knowing that his parents love each
other and they love him; he realizes that, in spite of small upsets, they are a happy family.

CHAPTER VII

Jealousy in the Oldest Child

IN DEALING with jealousy in the oldest child in the family we must recognize that he has been an only child until the arrival of the second-born. The chances are that he has been as jealous of his parents as the only child often is, and for the reasons mentioned in the last chapter. If his security has already been threatened by too many instances of real or imaginary loss of his parents' love, he will feel even more insecure when the baby arrives. He will look for—and he will find—evidence that the baby is depriving him of his mother's love, in the same way that his father deprived him of her love before the baby came.

Parents who have made some errors in bringing up an only child have another chance to straighten him out and help him restore his self-esteem when the new baby arrives. Unfortunately, they rarely know they are making mistakes; it's only after the child's problems show a crying need for a psychiatrist that parents may find out for the first time how they should have brought up their child. The greatest difficulty seems to lie in making the first-born king of the household and then, only too obviously, supplanting him with another object for their affections.

After all, for two to five or more years he has grown to bask in and need his parents' love. I don't know how sultans keep their first wife happy when they bring subsequent wives into the harem; the wives don't seem to be too perturbed, for the most part. I suppose, too, that the sultan forbids the wives to be jealous of each other. There are laws in this country prohibiting bigamy, but even if there weren't, only a very unreasonable husband could call his wife unreasonable because she happened to object to his bringing home another wife.

Imagine how unreasonable a child can get—and under what to him are identical circumstances. He will be jealous—he almost *has* to be—and one may as well know it and be prepared. Look for it in the first-born child and take care of it; all the rules apply. He must be told—and shown—that he is still loved; he must not be allowed to develop the feeling that he is being supplanted by the new baby; he shouldn't grow up hating the baby and resenting losing his parents' love. If he tries to win his parents' approval by becoming too involved in taking care of the baby, or by going into competition with her, one can be sure that the parents have made a mistake somewhere.

When any one of these things happens to a child it can be the reason for, or the result of, resentment—and naturally so. However, it is always essential to his future mental health that the resentment be brought out into the open. It does no one any good if the child's hatred of his rivals—his brothers or sisters—and his resentment against his parents is bottled up within him because of the threat of loss of approval. When it is, one can be sure it will come out in later years, not directed against those who inspired it, but against others who may be quite innocent victims of this unexpected hostility. There is a successful Broadway entertainer who had enough psychoanalysis to be able to mimic his elderly—and famous—Viennese analyst. "Remember," he will say, punctuating each word with a finger dug into your ribs, "you-are-never-hostile-to-the-one-who-is-present-at-the-time: it-is-really-someone-you-hate—" here he throws his body out of joint while he points violently to somewhere a mile or two behind him—"a-wa-a—a-a-a-y-back!"

It's decidedly better for a child to be allowed to express his feelings, even if it does sound offensive to his parents. For parents to be hurt because their son tells them the truth about themselves (as he sees it) shouldn't throw them into a panic. Too often it does. For example, a mother tries to put away her child's toys so that he will eat his dinner. He becomes furious and says, "You're nothing but an old meany and I hate you!" The mother should know that the child is thinking only of his own frustration, which he has a right to think of at his age, and so he hates her. If she is wise she will ignore the remark and try to mollify him while he gets into an eating mood; if she punishes him she convinces him that he is bad, and he begins to believe that only bad boys hate.

That was what happened to Donald Slattery. He was told, at an early age, that he must not hate. He loved his mother and she loved him; when he was seven, he begged and begged for a baby brother. He had no friends his own age and he was lonesome; he had no one but his parents and he spent his time shyly hanging on to his mother's apron. "He was scared of everyone and everything," his mother once said. "And then he got it into his head that he wanted a baby brother. I told him nothing doing—what was I going to say? And if we were going to have anything it would be a girl. Well, he carried on so, I had to explain to him that we didn't have any choice—that we had to take what came. So, you know what he said? 'Let's go down to the baby store; pick out the boy-baby parts and put them together ourselves.' Well, you should have heard my husband laugh at *that* one!"

Mrs. Slattery was not a heartless woman—far from it—although she gave the appearance of not caring. She was an average mother in the beginning; circumstances had made her bitter, and eventually she took out this bitterness on her children. Donald's father had died when he was five and his mother remarried when he was seven; after two years she had another son, Martin.

When Donald was eleven, Mrs. Slattery brought him to a mental-health clinic where arrangements are made for the mother to be interviewed by one psychiatric social worker at the same time that the child is seen by another psychiatric social worker.

To quote from the records of the social worker who saw Mrs. Slattery:

From the way the mother talks, I gather that the other children in the family are also a problem, but that Donald is the most difficult and has the added "evilness" of assuming that he is neglected and unloved. He is changeable, and she can't understand why it is that at home he is very sweet and lovable, while in school he is always getting into trouble. He told one of his teachers that nobody loved him. More recently he has become quite nasty to her, irritable and pouty, and he does exactly as he pleases, so that he has to be whipped frequently. Mrs. Slattery is mainly horrified that he still sucks his thumb.

Donald had a number of psychological tests which revealed that his intelligence was normal, among other things. The psychologist who gave the examination reported:

> He is a shy, retiring child who does not quite know what he can expect from his environment and is not ready to give much to others. He is tremendously suspicious and unable to take hold of new situations. His tendency is to hide and make himself inconspicuous. When he can withdraw to his rich inner life, he becomes freer and happier. There is a great deal of tension at all times, and this seems to arise out of a struggle in him which might be a struggle with people or a struggle to conquer life. . . . The child shows a good deal of mental health in that he is struggling and making an effort to get ahead; he is by no means passive and resigned. While this is encouraging, it does cause difficulties in getting along with people and an inability to give in and co-operate with others. He makes no effort to make a social adaptation, and all of his reactions are direct, self-centered, tense, and aggressive.

I won't go into great detail about all the interviews with Donald and his mother, but there are some things in the record that are interesting. One day when Donald came to the clinic he told Mrs. T., the psychiatric social worker, that his little half-brother Martin was waiting downstairs, and that Martin was jealous because he couldn't come in to talk to Mrs. T. To quote from the record:

Donald says that he wishes he lived across the street, so that he could come over here all the time and stay all day. He looks at the nursing bottle suddenly and says, "Who is that for?" I tell him that it is for him, if he wants to use it. "Can I drink water out of it?" he asks. I tell him he can, and I tell him where he can fill it. He comes back into the room, sits down, and begins to suck on the bottle, then stops and says that he would like to show it to Martin. He goes downstairs and takes the bottle with him, shows Martin the bottle very proudly, and tells him that he can drink out of it if he wants to but that Martin can't. He comes upstairs with Martin, sits down, and begins to suck on the bottle, saying to Martin, "Look, look at what I'm doing!" Martin is looking at him quite enviously, and then begins to look over the toys. He grabs a piece of candy, and Donald says that he can't do that. I have some trouble getting Martin out of the room finally.

Again Donald asks me about the children who come to the Clinic and why they come. He asks me about the little boy who comes in when he is leaving. They pass each other but ignore each other, I have noticed. He volunteers the information that he has been getting along much better in school and he is trying harder to be good. I ask him how he has been getting along with his mother, and he says, very philosophically, "Oh, Mother and I fight all the time," as though there isn't much that can be done about it one way or the other.

He decides to get more water in the bottle, and when he returns he sucks on the nipple very aggressively. At the end of the hour he again takes candy. When he leaves the building, he stands outside in the alley and calls to me, asking who is in the room with me. The boy who is in the room goes to the window, and he and Donald make faces at one another.

Now turning to the interview the following week between Mrs. Slattery and *her* social worker, Mrs. V., here is the record, as Mrs. V. wrote it:

Mrs. Slattery tells me that she had whaled the stuffing out of Donald and Martin because they lied about what hap-

pened in the Clinic. She says: "God damn, I forgot to call
that Mrs. T.; I meant to call her during the week, and I forgot. I don't know what I do with my mind or if I laid it
away. What do you think those little imps have been saying? I know perfectly well that it isn't true; that Mrs. T. is
certainly no dumbbell, and she would never think of saying
or doing such a thing. I must say I am surprised because I
never caught Donald in a lie before, and that happens to be
one of the things my children don't do: they don't lie. . . ."
And on and on and on, until I interrupt and say, "What
in the world is it that Donald has said and done, and what
is this about Mrs. T.? What is it that you want to say to
her?"

Mrs. Slattery then says that Donald has been telling everybody—and it's just full of a pack of lies—that Mrs. T. had
been giving him a nursing bottle. By the time Mrs. Slattery
gets to saying this, she is full of apologies, assuring me that
it is absurd, that Mrs. T. would not have done such a thing,
and she knows very well it is all Donald. I interrupt her to
say that there are two things I would like to tell her: the
first, in answer to her obvious question as to whether Mrs.
T. gave Donald a nursing bottle, I tell her that I expect she
probably did; that there is a nursing bottle there, and the
children do enjoy sucking on it. I tell her that I can see she
has a great many questions about the advisability of this and
that we will discuss it.

I also tell her that I think we ought to discuss all this talk
about "Donald must be a liar and Mrs. T. must be right."
Mother says, "Well, my God, why a nursing bottle? All these
years, eleven years old, he should be over sucking on a bottle. If you knew all the time I've put into getting him to
take his finger out of his mouth, it drives me nuts, I tell
you. I've tried everything to get that finger out of his mouth.
I've thought of tying it up, of putting his arm in a sling, and
then people always say, 'Stop them from sucking their fingers and maybe they'll do worse things.' And here all these
years of effort to get his finger out of his mouth, and why
should he want a nursing bottle? Why should he want his
finger in his mouth? There must be something the matter
with the child."

"You are very decidedly right, Mrs. Slattery," I tell her. "There is something the matter with this child. It's obvious that you feel very upset because you think we are encouraging the thumb-sucking habit by giving Donald the nursing bottle. I want to assure you that our goal is to help Donald overcome it. We intend doing it not by training him or untraining him about his thumb, but by considering that a child of eleven who sucks his thumb as much as Donald does is certainly a very anxious child, and that there is something the matter with him. You must have realized that there was something the matter with him when you came to the Clinic and asked for help." I feel that I managed to get her out of her tizzy about Donald being given a bottle here in the Clinic, and into the business of whether or not this encouraged Donald in a habit which his mother is trying to break him of. I talk pretty much about Donald having a need to suck on something and that if in his hour here he sucks on a bottle it might do something to relieve his necessity to suck on his thumb. I explain to her that we do not attempt to train children here in what is right or wrong; that is the mother's business. "We are here," I tell her, "only to help a child who seems to be upset and nervous and highstrung, to get at his problem so that he may be able to be a happy and better adjusted child." Mrs. Slattery is silent for a second and then says, "I guess I can see that. After all, I guess you know your business. . . ."

There were more interviews with Donald, interviews which brought out that Donald used to sleep with his mother, after his own father died. He talked freely about his love for his mother, and before he actually came out and told about his hatred for his real father, he began to ask a number of questions such as, "Is it really all right to hate somebody you don't like?"

Mrs. T. answered him: "First you have to find out why you don't like the person."

"Well, like when you think they're the favorite, and when you think they get all the fun."

"Like Martin?" Mrs. T. asked him.

"Yes, like Martin. He gets away with everything 'cause he's the littlest."

"You mean that your mother loves him more than she loves you. Isn't that it?"

"Yes, I guess that's it."

It took some time before Donald was able to connect his hatred for his father, stepfather, and half-brother to his feeling that his mother had loved them more than she loved him. They were depriving him of something that he felt was rightly his. He was jealous of them because they had what he didn't have. It was necessary to show Donald that if he really felt unloved he had a right to hate and that he wasn't the most vicious person in the world just because he hated an injustice.

A person who hates is a person who feels hated; this isn't one of the emotions that a child is proud of. It helps to confirm his feelings of low self-esteem: he thinks that he is worthless and a bad person. This was exaggerated in Donald's case because he had the impression that his hatred of his own father was such a potent thing that it caused his father's death. Obviously, Donald would get the most benefit from his treatment in the clinic if he were permitted to be resentful whenever he felt that his mother loved him less or loved others more than she loved him. When he got the impression that his resentment was not wrong, he began to dislike himself less. Meanwhile, as treatment progressed, his mother began to undertake more and more of the responsibilities in the home; she began to realize that one of her responsibilities was to make up to Donald for the love she had not given him.

Sometimes the feeling of jealousy shows up as something very pleasing; at least it's pleasing to the parents. They see their oldest child, for instance, displaying great sympathy, kindness, and solicitude for the younger child, or even children, to the point where the oldest child takes over completely and serves as an assistant parent. What may happen in such cases is this: the child *is* jealous, but he tries to push the jealous feelings out of his conscious mind. It's a "bad" feeling, this jealousy, and he may have learned it is "bad" because he

was once punished for showing his real feelings. So he re-
places his "bad" feelings—or atones for them—by being self-
sacrificing and showing how kind and generous he can be.

It's interesting that so many of the "oldest" children don't
marry; in family after family the oldest son or oldest daughter plays papa or mama, sitting back and beaming as the
younger brothers and sisters leave to get married. It isn't only
self-sacrifice: when the younger children all leave home it
leaves the oldest in charge, once more the most important
member of the household. Surprisingly enough, this is closely
related to his jealousy when the other children arrived: it is
the wish to have his parents to himself. Some thirty years
later his wish comes true: he is the only child again.

Parents may welcome the oldest child's taking over their
own duties; they expect it if the oldest child is a girl. The
child does it to get approval. She may become extremely
bitter or extremely submissive; she may not go to either extreme. However, there is rarely a family in which the oldest
takes over that doesn't show some bad aftereffects on either
the oldest child or the children she is presumably taking care
of. Grace Landers and Sally Kuhn were two examples of such
bitterness and oversubmissiveness.

Grace Landers was bitter about being the deputy parent.
She was five when the first of her two sisters was born. Still
later a brother was born. Her mother was what one might
call "devoted to her children"; she pounced on each new
child to the exclusion of the older ones. Thus while Mrs.
Landers was so completely preoccupied with each newborn
infant, Grace took charge of the upbringing of the others—
out of sheer resentment. Her mother was involved with the
baby; Grace hated it—hated losing her mother and hated
being left in the lurch.

When she first went to a psychiatrist Grace Landers was an
imperious, hostile, and efficient woman. After seventeen years'
apprenticeship running her younger brother and sisters, she
graduated with honors from a nurses' training school. She
won a scholarship in administrative practice, which was a

waste because she had spent all those years becoming an administrator. She never went into actual nursing, but became the supervisor of nurses at a local hospital; by the time she was forty she was superintendent of a large hospital. There she earned a reputation for efficiency which was only matched by her reputation for heartlessness. She was cold and empty. She allowed herself no softness or warmth. Her job was her life. Somewhere she had learned that the best way to deal with people was to waste no sympathy on them and never to be tender.

After all, why should she have been kind? Who was ever kind to her? She had spent her life bringing up her brother and sisters with only one motive behind it: it was a way to get ahead. It was the only way she could hold on to her parents' love; it was necessary for her to do a good job as deputy parent in order to get their approval. This was exactly the same as the way she functioned in her business life: she did an excellent job as administrator, not for her personal satisfaction, but to gain the approval of her superiors first.

Well, eventually people who are so fantastically successful run out of superiors: they have no more sources of approval; they are faced with themselves and their lack of satisfactions. They say to themselves, "Who am I? What am I doing here? Why am I not happy? What am I doing unmarried?" They become aware of the emptiness which is so common among the unloved ones, who are so because they can't love. Grace Landers felt this unhappiness and depression; she thought at first it was premature menopause and made the rounds of the specialists on the staff of the hospital. They said it wasn't; to a man they recommended that she see a psychiatrist. When she finally did go to one she learned for the first time how she was still maintaining her childish need for approval, and that she had always felt herself forsaken by her parents. There is a happy ending to this story: Grace married, at forty-four, a widower with three children. She loves her husband and she loves his children; what is always so surprising to her former colleagues is that her husband and the children love her.

What went wrong that made Grace Landers so successful and so cold? She was an only child for five years; she was dethroned when the first sister arrived. It was as if she had literally been given her walking papers. Her mother was so engrossed in each new baby that she didn't pay attention to the effect on the other—the older—children, most especially on Grace. During her psychoanalysis Grace remembered that when the baby was born she was sent off to kindergarten: she felt as if she were being exiled. She wanted her home and her parents' love so badly that she made a fuss about not wanting to go to school; she was accused of being a jealous child. This was disapproval, to be sure; there was more disapproval when the baby was loved and she was neglected. She resolved to get back into her parents' good graces by making herself invaluable to her mother, so she helped her by taking over the upbringing of the other children. She got her approval, all right; at the same time she worked up a lot of hostility out of resentment against her role: she went on to become efficient and bitter—it was by then a habit of living.

Her mother made her first mistake when she was so very obvious about loving the new baby. She made the next mistake in sending Grace to kindergarten to get her out of the house. The third mistake was the *accusation* that Grace was jealous, so that Grace was sure she would be loved less for being jealous. This failure to permit Grace to be jealous was the most serious mistake her mother made.

Sally Kuhn is now forty-two, a noble, unselfish, and self-sacrificing person, whose life was filled with her duties to her younger brothers and sisters. She was eighteen when her mother died; she had three younger brothers, the youngest two years old, and two younger sisters. Even before the death of her mother, Sally took over the care of the Kuhn brood. *She* didn't go to high school, but the other children did; *she* made sure the two older boys went to college, too. When their father became sick and there was no money left, Sally went to work and put the two boys through law school; the others at least made a stab at doing what they wanted. The youngest boy is now in college and the two sisters are happily married.

Sally may be happy as she sits in her room alone at night, thinking of the nice dinner she had at the home of one or the other of the younger Kuhns, but then again she may not be. Many women deny themselves normal satisfactions and pleasures and sacrifice their entire lives to their younger brothers or sisters. It is as if they were doing lifelong penance for an unworthy feeling which they can never forget. Very often, while they are doing so much good, they resent the people for whom they sacrifice themselves.

This is the vicious circle of resentment which we want to avoid by recognizing jealousy when it exists. I hope I have made a little more clear the theory that jealousy itself isn't harmful—but the resentment which it creates may be a life-long attitude. It may be expressed (Grace Landers became a martinet) or it may be repressed (Sally Kuhn punished herself). Today, very few older children are as self-sacrificing as Sally was. There are smaller families, for one thing, and it is possible to plan children so that mothers can take care of each baby without feeling overly burdened with work. Most parents today prefer to give each child a chance to have an education and a life of his or her own.

There isn't much a parent can do to avoid jealousy in the oldest child except to play down the importance of the new baby. Unfortunately this may lead to trouble, too, because it can be overdone and the baby will suffer. When parents are sure that the baby won't be hurt by it, they can ease the older one's troubles immeasurably. One should think of it this way: there is no way in the world to make the older child understand that his parents weren't supplanting him when they had the baby. They can do only two things. They can ease the shock somewhat and they can let him express himself openly.

He needs to verbalize his feelings and he should be permitted to be jealous. Parents might try having private talks with him, not probing or questioning, but explaining to him that they understand his feelings and they know that he can't help them. "We know how you feel; we understand; we still love you very much, and we want you just as much as ever. If you do feel unhappy or hurt, or if you hate us once in a while, come and tell us; we know that you can't help feeling that way and we know you're not a bad boy." Once is not enough. He should be told again and again, preferably at a time when his mother or father is alone with him, when he won't be ashamed to cry or to express his real feelings.

He shouldn't be made to feel that the baby is in any way a burden to him, or his responsibility. Parents should try especially hard not to let the baby's routine interfere with the routine he has established. They shouldn't goad him by questions such as "Do you like the new baby?" He is too mixed up to know whether he does or not. Any time parents show extra pleasure in the new baby it should be classified under the heading of "Cruelty to the Oldest Child."

Mother should let the older child help her, if he wants, with other chores, such as cooking or setting the table, but she shouldn't insist on his helping with the baby. She should have friends around for him, make his parties important, let him have a room that is filled with *his* things. He shouldn't be allowed to go away and sulk in silence; he needs help and patience and understanding and he never should be ignored, even accidentally.

His mother will probably have to take many derogatory comments on herself. He'll say "You're mean," when she was just faintly suggesting that he do something; "You hate me," when she asks him to put away his toys, or "I hate you," when she just has to put him to bed. She should be as understanding as she possibly can and reassure him constantly. He wants to make her unhappy because he feels that she has made him miserable.

In effect I seem to be encouraging maliciousness, revenge, hatred, bitterness, and other aspects of jealousy in children: I do this because we are talking about children. These are emotions which are normal for children; like training pants, they should be used up and not needed when the children reach adulthood.

CHAPTER VIII

Jealousy in the Second Child of Two

JEALOUSY occurs most frequently in the first-born child, chiefly because he had been so used to the privileges and benefits of being an only child. But what about the younger one, the second child? His status—he is the baby of the family —makes him the object of the older child's resentment, while he himself may well be resentful of the older child's apparent advantages.

The older child, at the time, is the stronger one, and he won't willingly or readily give up his own possessions. And in addition, he can usually take for himself any of the younger one's things, whenever he wants to. It isn't easy to handle the problem, especially when the baby knows that he will be protected; he very quickly learns that the world he lives in is made up of people who just love to come to the aid of the helpless.

As a general rule one can expect that the more important problem is that of the older child's jealousy: the younger one does get more attention and feels more secure. With this principle in mind Mrs. Mountain solved what might have turned out to be very serious difficulties between her two sons. She is a war widow; at the time she asked a psychiatrist for help her son Alfred was six and Hugh was four. She was rather upset because she wasn't sure that she could bring the children up without a father. The psychoanalyst was impressed with her unwillingness to believe that she was a good mother; it seemed to him, from the way she described her children's

problems and the way she handled them, that she was doing
an excellent job. Her problem was, as it turned out, a lack
of appreciation of her own abilities, which were considerable.

"She made a very complete study of children," her doctor
told me, "and she had a better understanding of them than
most mothers. She is a wonderful example of the value of an
education in child care."

One day she came late; she told him that a fight broke out
between the boys and she wanted to see it settled before she
left.

"Was it a bad fight?" the doctor asked her.

"No," Mrs. Mountain said, "they only slap. They really
don't want to hurt each other, just to let off steam. They
usually work it out themselves. There's plenty of time to step
in and stop them—I keep an eye on them to see that they
don't hurt each other seriously. Also, I make sure that Hugh
isn't permitted to get away with too much—I don't protect
him if I can help it. The only way he'll learn to respect
Alfred's property is by my letting Alfred smack him down
occasionally.

"I know I sound bloodthirsty," she continued, "but I think
that there are less fights now that Hugh knows he can't steal
Alfred's toys. Hugh wants an electric train. Alfred has one
and Hugh is making a big fuss. So I will compromise: I'll buy
Hugh a small mechanical train—and I'll explain to him that
he isn't big enough to get an electric train."

"And he won't feel frustrated?" the doctor asked.

"He only wants the train because he wants to compete with
Alfred," Mrs. Mountain said. "He'll be more frustrated if I
get him a train that he can't cope with. As it is he knows he
can trust me, so he'll be satisfied to have a mechanical train—
any kind for now—because he knows he'll get a bigger one
when he grows up.

"I try to make Hugh respect the older one's possessions and
I don't baby him. It's more important to assure Alfred that
his things will be safe than it is to give in to Hugh. So I
reassure Alfred whenever I can because he's more apt to be

jealous. Hugh is younger, and he gets more attention and love anyway."

If there is any rule about jealousy in children that could be called basic, it's what Mrs. Mountain said about Hugh: because he's younger he gets more love and attention than the older brother. The one most important thing to remember when handling the problem of jealousy in the older child is this: parents can probably never make up to him for having another child. It means that the love the younger one gets (because he is younger) ought to be enough for him to coast on while his parents give the older child a larger portion. Perhaps it's possible to neglect the younger child; perhaps it might even be beneficial to the older one, but where does one stop? How can one tell when the neglect will affect the younger child? If the older child doesn't have to work out his resentment on the younger one it will be better for both of them. But at any time that the younger child begins to notice the advantages the older one enjoys, he may become jealous.

This happened to the children of the Parkers, a well-meaning couple who had two sons, Stuart and David. Stuart was born when his father was in the army and he was brought up in the officers' quarters at an army camp. When the war was over the Parkers moved in with Mrs. Parker's family; David was born there. Stuart was two and a half years old at the time. From the beginning David was in trouble with his grandparents: he cried at night.

They were two nice old people, those grandparents, except that in the twenty odd years that had elapsed since their youngest child stopped crying they had become very insistent on peace and quiet in the night. They became highly critical of David—and his mother—but very fond of Stuart. This one, even if he had wanted to cry, didn't, because crying meant disapproval. Mrs. Parker became much too sensitive about David's occasional cries.

When Stuart was six and David was almost four the Parkers found a place to live by themselves; they settled down and tried to repair the damage that had been done their children.

The damage consisted of the following: Stuart was a bed wetter and thumb sucker, while David was a tantrum thrower. Peculiarly enough, David only threw tantrums when the grandparents were around. The doctor whom the Parkers consulted explained how the extra attention paid David by Mrs. Parker led Stuart to believe he should be a child again; hence the bed wetting and thumb sucking. David was showing his extreme resentment of his brother Stuart's favored position with his grandparents by trying to get attention; hence the temper tantrums.

The Parkers began a very careful campaign to correct their mistakes. No more babying for Stuart. Both children were sent to day nurseries and both were encouraged to make friends for themselves alone. Their relatives and friends were told to pay a lot of attention to David, and everything seemed to be working out fine, when suddenly one day there came a number of very expensive gifts for Stuart from—yes, that's right—the grandparents. Just their way of announcing their arrival for a visit a few days later. It forced the harassed and not too wealthy Parkers into buying somewhat similar and equally expensive gifts for David to make it up to him. Also, it prompted them to write a firm, polite, but pointed letter to the old people telling them what they could and could not say or do when—and if—they visited.

The Parkers have achieved excellent results by having done a good job. David never has to wear any of Stuart's castoff clothing, nor does he have to content himself with Stuart's played-out toys. His bike isn't as big as Stuart's but it's as new and shiny. The security of both children shows: they have fun with their own friends, they like each other—and fight each other, too—and they don't wet beds, suck their thumbs, or throw tantrums.

The case of Vickie Turner comes to mind. She grew up to be a tomboy because she was jealous of her older brother: he stole her parents' love away from her, even though he did it in self-defense. Her jealousy took the form of resentment that she was a girl. By the time she was thirteen she was a behavior problem. She was backward in her schoolwork and involved with some juvenile delinquents. She wasn't a slum child. Her background was surprisingly good. Her parents were college graduates and they were well off even if they weren't wealthy. Vickie was a misfit in her family as well as in her gang: she wasn't the type that the boys in the gangs like to have around. They were suspicious at first, but when she began to show them that she could beat them at their own games they gave in.

She had an older brother, Chet, who was four years old when she was born; he reacted to her arrival by feeling rejected and displaced. He was jealous of her. At the age of four a child naturally begins to make friends with other children; he is well on the way to breaking some of the closer ties to his mother. Sometimes this doesn't happen, as when a new baby arrives: the threat of the loss of his mother's love may make him want to stay close to home. He may feel that in this way he can keep an eye on the enemy and forestall him; besides, he can get in some of his own bids for attention. But there are some who don't react that way: they feel rejected at home and attempt to make up for the loss of parental love by seeking companionship on the outside.

That was what Vickie's brother did. He had many friends among the children in the neighborhood, and later on in school, and he made himself outstanding. He had to, it would seem, because he wasn't made to feel important at home—they went and got themselves Vickie—and he had to feel important somewhere else, in order to feel worth while. In the course of his rise to such success with his fellows he became increasingly popular with his parents; they were proud of him when he was six, a better athlete than most eight-year-olds, and better liked than most children in their part of town. Vickie was two, still adored by her parents, but becoming aware that something was threatening her accustomed security. More and more praise went to her brother; this meant she was getting less, as time went on, although she wasn't really thought less of, nor loved less, than she had been. Nevertheless she thought she was, because she heard her brother praised.

From her subsequent behavior it would seem that her brother's aggressiveness was infectious, because she became aggressive, too, but in an unpleasing and unbecoming way. First she grew more demanding: she insisted on being around her mother all the time and would start to scream if Mrs. Turner even so much as tried to leave her alone. When Mr. Turner came home at night she would climb into his lap and try to monopolize all of his attention; he had great difficulty carrying on a conversation with anyone, especially her brother. It was unfortunate that these excessive bids for approval were not recognized and understood by her parents. In fact, the very worst things that could have happened took place from the time she was two years old.

The martyred mother couldn't even leave her daughter with the neighbors when she went to the store and she began to dislike the child more and more. Also, she felt guilty, because a good mother isn't supposed to dislike her children. By the time Vickie was four she hadn't yet been completely toilet-trained—she still wet her bed regularly—and—she asked questions. We should expect children to be curious about things, and we should expect they will ask questions, but only now and then. We should also know that they may ask the same questions over and over again, and we shouldn't get too impatient or think that our children are less bright than we had expected. However, there is a limit beyond which even the most patient and understanding mother cannot go, and Mrs. Turner had been pushed beyond that saturation point. Here is an abbreviated version of what went on:

"Where is Daddy?" Vickie would start off with this question each morning, about half an hour after Mr. Turner had left the house.

"He went to the office," her mother would say.

"Why?"

"To work there. He works in the office."

"Why? Why does he work there?"

"Because he has to make money."

"Why does he?"

"Everybody does. He has to do it so that I can buy things to eat and dresses for you."

"Why doesn't he make money at home?"

"His work is at his office. . . . Now listen Vickie: I told you all of this yesterday, and now I have work to do. I have to clean up the kitchen. Go play with your doll."

"I don't want to. I want Daddy to work here. Why does he have to go away?"

At this point Mrs. Turner, depending on her mood and the length of time the grilling had been going on, would either resist the temptation or say, with somewhat justifiable emphasis, "Because he's luckier than I am." It did no good: Vickie would want to know why, if Mummy could do *her* work in the kitchen, Daddy couldn't do his in the kitchen, too. Or, why didn't Mummy work in an office? Or, why couldn't Daddy take Vickie with him? It wasn't at all helpful, either, to question Vickie:

"Didn't I tell you yesterday where Daddy went?" Mrs. Turner might ask. "Now think, Vickie. Where did he go yesterday?"

Quick as a flash would come the answer: "I don't know. Where did Daddy go yesterday?"

Vickie became less endearing, as you might expect, because her mother, instead of trying to find out what bothered her child, became annoyed at her symptoms. Vickie's excessive questioning was part of her plan to get attention (which meant love) by "testing" her mother. Not that she was grading Mrs. Turner according to the accuracy of her answers, but testing to see if her mother still loved her. This is a favorite device of children, and it makes life a trial for their parents. They do things, not consciously perhaps, which cause their parents great displeasure, because they want to see how far they can go—and still be loved. Vickie needed to know she was loved because she was becoming increasingly aware that her older brother was getting some of her parents' affection.

Excessive questioning by a child can nearly always be put down to the child's need for reassurance, a need for security. But make sure first that it's excessive. What may seem to be an abnormal amount of inquisitiveness could very well be the normal quest for knowledge in a child; sometimes parents will have to ask themselves: "Am I just too impatient?" No matter if the parent is convinced that it *is* abnormal, or isn't too sure, there is no immediate cure; also, the correct way to handle it is not to discourage the child, or to show impatience, or to punish or scold. Ideally, the solution should consist of taking care of what bothers the child: find out why the child should feel insecure and do something about *that*. Also, look for other evidences of insecurity; you will find that excessive questioning is not the only way in which the child shows that it is feeling unloved, or unsure of its parents' love.

Sometimes a mother can prove that the child isn't asking an abnormal number of questions by devoting part of the morning—a half hour, or even less—to a sort of domestic quiz program, in which the mother shows a real—to the child— interest in the child's questions. This is done by actually taking time out from her other duties to show the child that she is ready to answer questions—to give helpful information, and not merely to repeat absent-minded, weary replies that may not have satisfied the child the first time she asked the questions. When Vickie asked where Daddy went, Mrs. Turner could have said, "He went to work in an office. An office is a large room, with desks in it. A desk is like a table. Your daddy sits at the desk. He works at the desk. He reads letters and he writes letters. He talks to other people. . . ." And so on, depending on Vickie's intelligence and understanding. Of course, these statements may have to be repeated a number of times, too, but at least you are honest about it and giving the child information. Also, the child who asks questions merely for the sake of asking questions—that sometimes happens—will get bored with such explanatory answers long before the mother gets tired of making them.

The Turners saw no significance in Vickie's persistent questioning, but decided that she was a pest. They didn't connect it up with her destructiveness (her toys and dolls were apparently the most fragile in the world), her eating habits (she had a most delicate appetite and could hardly eat anything), or her aforementioned bed wetting. They became annoyed at her, while at the same time they were getting to be prouder and prouder of their son: he was everything that Vickie was not. Soon they began to tell Vickie so, by comparing her to Chet. They told her she wasn't as careful with her things as he was, that she wasn't as obedient, that *Chet* didn't wet his bed, and hundreds of other things. They didn't know that it was a vicious thing to do: they thought they would be teaching her to behave, by pointing out that they preferred behavior like her brother's.

Vickie could have retired from the combat; she could have decided to give up, leaving the field to her brother. Sometimes children do, as I explain in the chapter dealing with comparing children to each other. But Vickie didn't give up, exactly; she decided to obey her parents: if what they wanted was someone who behaved like her brother, she would be a boy, too. . . . For the next nine years she put on an imitation of her brother that went so far beyond merely being a tomboy that she ended up just short of being a juvenile delinquent. She became less and less feminine, less girlish, and less appealing to her parents, which was exactly the opposite of the effect she wanted to create.

Why didn't she imitate Chet's good qualities? Why did she become antisocial? She might have turned out differently except for the mistakes her family made, mistakes they weren't aware of. She wanted her parents' love and tried hard to get it by imitating her brother. When she found that it did no good, that they loved her even less, she became bitter: she gave in to her growing conviction that she was bad, an idea that her parents implanted in her as surely as if they had been deliberate and vicious, which they were not.

Vickie was no more possessive and demanding of love than other babies, but she got less love because her mother unconsciously held herself back. Vickie had to begin to think of herself as an inadequate child, else how could she explain her parents' preference for her brother? She was convinced that she was inadequate when she began to believe that she was bad. A number of things happened which made her think so.

First, and most obvious, she had heard her mother say: "You are a bad girl, Vickie" enough times to begin to believe that this was one of the reasons she wasn't loved. She didn't differ much from other children in her interpretation.

Second, she began to believe that everything she did was tainted by her badness. For example, she had a vivid imagination, so she loved to embroider stories about commonplace incidents. Her parents didn't understand that she was driven to these fantasies because of the loneliness, the unlovedness, of her real life, and labeled the stories lies. Lying, Vickie knew, was something only bad girls did.

Third (and this is something which occurs only too frequently because parents are not willing to explain sex to their children), Vickie thought she had lost her penis. She wondered why Chet had one and she didn't have one; she had no way of knowing that boys have them and girls don't, that it was natural and normal. She hit on an explanation which is unfortunately much too prevalent among little girls: she figured out that she had one once, but she had lost it because she was bad. This thought was buried in her unconscious, but it may have contributed to her decision to become a tomboy: acting like a boy would compensate for the loss of her penis. After all, if one has all the external appearance and adopts the behavior of a boy, who is going to think that one has no penis?

Vickie became a tomboy not only for this reason, or because it seemed to her that boys get more privileges, more freedom, and more love than girls; there was still another important factor involved. In the process of identification—or imitation—the child may choose as a model the favorite parent, or the parent whose approval means more. Perhaps the Oedipal situation made her father the more important figure to Vickie; at any rate we mustn't overlook the possibility that imitating him could have been one more reason for Vickie's becoming a tomboy.

Vickie was too much for her parents to handle. Fortunately for the family, they eventually recognized it and sent her to a psychiatrist, where all these things were discussed with her. She did a lot of talking because she wasn't afraid to tell about her real feelings, something she hadn't been permitted to do at home. In this way the doctor was able to learn her story and interpret it, so that she and her family were able to find out what was going on. Knowing that her misbehavior was really the acting out of her jealousy and resentment was a big help in getting Vickie to give up her antisocial activities. Knowing, too, that she wasn't "born bad," and that she was only acting that way because she was afraid that she couldn't possibly change, was even more important.

Mrs. Turner was made aware of her own problems by the psychiatrist; she and her husband began to see that their daughter needed more understanding, security, companionship at home—and love. It took time, months and months, while Vickie and her mother cautiously began to try trusting each other; after that came an acceptance of each other which can only occur when two people really begin to understand themselves. Vickie, knowing she was loved, no longer had to compete with her brother; she was able to drop her gang play and live more like a happy, well-adjusted person.

When we discuss jealousy between two or more children in a family we call it sibling rivalry, because it refers to the competition between them. They compete for their parents' approval, which means they compete for favors, compliments, smiles, rewards, ice cream, or being allowed to go next door to watch the television. When one child consistently wins out over another for these things, it is because they have been placed in competition with each other by their parents. If parents emphasize competitiveness in their children it becomes so much a part of their lives that they may grow up eternally trying to be better than a sibling in order to win recognition. This kind of competition often leads to self-defeat, because every situation becomes a competitive one and the individual's energies are always turned to trying to be better than someone else.

Where there is sibling rivalry there is also discontent, and it's very hard to eliminate it. Parents must train themselves to be absolutely fair in dealing with the problems that arise between the children: they should be very sparing of blame or praise. They should encourage each child to work hard at something that he's capable of doing, but they shouldn't emphasize one child's ability so much that they shut out recognition of the other one's accomplishments.

Success isn't a matter of how much better you are than the next fellow: he may be a failure. Success is the knowledge one has that he has done his work to the best of his abilities. A mature person is one who as a child learned these things: that winning a game is less important than the fun of playing it; that high marks in school are less important than learning what he studies, and that happiness doesn't mean that he has to be the best there is. There could very well be a lot of contentment in a world that is less competitive. However, that would require that competition's beginnings, sibling rivalry, be eliminated in the home, if at all possible. It's a very difficult job, and what makes it harder is the ease with which all the good work parents do at home can be wiped out by the emphasis on competition in school, on playgrounds, and later on at work.

CHAPTER IX

Jealousy in the Second Child of Three

THERE are not too great problems with jealousy in the second child of two children; for the most part, as we have seen, the baby gets more attention and love. The older child is most frequently the jealous one: one must handle his problems first, so that his symptoms won't cause too much trouble for the younger one. It has been shown that the oldest child in the family of three children can be just as jealous as when he was the older child of two children. The difference is this: sometimes he may welcome the third child as an ally against the second child, someone who may even help him get even with Number Two. It's as deliberate, sometimes, as all that.

The child who is caught in the middle is naturally the one who is going to suffer: when he was the baby of the family, when there were only two children, he had certain privileges which he enjoyed. He came to expect that they would continue, that he would always be favored because he was the baby. He suffers because the older one resents him, but he suffers more when he is replaced in his parents' affection by a new arrival. In this the attitude of the parents can be most helpful. The second child's jealousy of the new baby is a problem which is every bit as urgent as the jealousy of the oldest child when the second child was born. Three children now have to be loved equally; a mother has to be three times as tender and understanding.

As I pointed out, the older child can be so resentful of the second one that he may join forces with the third child, the baby. He welcomes the new baby; he looks forward to its arrival with even more interest than he showed when the second child was expected. It may be that he is even gloating and gleeful that the second child is being fired from his job as baby in the family, because he remembers what happened to himself when he was fired. In any event, the child in the middle gets it from both sides, and will show it almost from the beginning. The actual plot against him may not unfold until much later in life, when it's too late to do anything about it. And sometimes there is no plot at all: it's all imagined by the second child, who says his unhappiness is due to the fact that the older child and the younger one are against him.

To sum up the special problems which face the second child in the family of three (or more) children, first: he is faced with the loss of his advantages as the baby; second: he is the object of the older one's resentment; and third: he may fall victim of a coalition between the older and younger children. It goes without saying that in the middle of all this he is just plain jealous of the new baby.

Take these difficulties, which are part of the hazards of being the second child, then add some lack of understanding by his parents, and one has a problem with jealousy. Further complicate it and you have the story of Eric, who was the second of three children. His father was an architect and industrial designer; he had been an artist—a modern artist— when he was younger, and his modern factories, as well as his designs for industrial products, were highly thought of. The oldest boy was Harold, four years older than Eric; Jane was three years younger than Eric.

There was no particular trouble with Eric at home, at least none that made his parents worry. At his day school, which he entered when he was almost six, it was noticed that he was "slow" and "lazy." Now these words, when used by the careful and observant teachers at this private school, were not spoken lightly. They were an accurate description of Eric after he had been there for six months. In the first place, he was so very different from Harold, who was a bright, quick, athletic lad, excelling in many things. But it wasn't only these differences that might have exaggerated the contrast between the two boys: Eric was less capable of making an adjustment than the other children. The fact is that he was noticeably peculiar.

He didn't play games very often, but when he did he played with the girls' groups rather than with the boys'. He wasn't well dressed; he had to wear his older brother's hand-me-downs, and he had grown too tall for the clothes to be any longer fashionable or esthetic. His hair was long, almost as long as a girl's. He never made belts in class, but would use the ribbons to tie around him; he liked to make bows for himself to wear. He was Daddy when he and the girls played house. He wept easily, so he wept often; he ran and he threw a ball in a manner best described as effeminate.

Mrs. Fane, his teacher, talked it over with the head of the school, and Eric's mother was called in for a conference. (This is a happy thing; I approve of schools that don't mind telling parents the truth about themselves and their children.) Eric's mother and father were both told about the situation and seemed surprised. They hadn't noticed anything remarkable about his behavior at home. They wondered if the school wasn't exaggerating somewhat.

"You have so many unusual children here," Eric's father said. "All of the geniuses in New York, if they're any sort of geniuses at all, send their children to you. I hate to say it—and I don't want you to think that I'm being insulting—but Eric is probably normal, and maybe that's what confuses you."

It was the usual defensiveness of parents. Eric's teacher, Mrs. Fane, and Mrs. Thomas, the principal, looked as if they were sighing wearily and didn't press the point. Eric continued in school. That summer he and Harold went to the camp run by the school and here Mrs. Fane saw him growing more and more girllike. Again he stayed away from the boys and played, when he played, with the girls. At the end of the summer, because his parents hadn't returned from Europe, Mrs. Fane took both boys home with her. She had two daughters, one Eric's age; both girls went to the same school and had been at camp, too. Mrs. Fane discovered that Eric liked to wear girls' clothes: he made it a game, to be sure, and it was all innocent, but it seemed that he always wanted to play just those games in which he had to wear girls' clothes.

Back at school Eric was still somewhat backward. He didn't learn to read as well as the other children, nor was he anywhere near his age group in the other school activities. However, he did learn to sew and cook, and was very good at these things. About this time his little sister Jane was entered in kindergarten. She was just like Harold, only much more alive, vital, and demanding. Mrs. Fane said one day, watching Jane and Eric together during a play period: "She talks and does for both of them." Jane wore pretty clothes, the prettiest in the school; very often Eric would go over to her while she was playing and straighten a bow or a pleat in her dress, or brush her hair straight with his hand.

There had been no word from his parents about any problems with him at home, and Mrs. Fane felt somewhat dejected. She felt that Eric needed help. She did what she could: she gave him more attention than she gave other children, encouraged him, tried to get him to make some response, to come alive, but it wasn't too successful. She wanted desperately to find out what troubled the boy, but couldn't without his parents' help. Then one day she got a phone call from Eric's mother. She wanted to come to see Mrs. Fane and talk to her about Eric. Mrs. Fane thought, "At last! Now we'll be able to do something about the boy!"

It wasn't going to be that simple, unfortunately. Eric's mother came to school with a large folder which had some pictures in tempera and some water colors. They were remarkable pictures, Mrs. Fane thought, and much better than those usually painted by children. They were Eric's. Children don't paint as accurately as Eric; they are of the expressionistic school, usually, while Eric had produced work which was definitely of the academic school. His work showed remarkable talent: there was an almost photographic quality about it. Mrs. Fane thought his mother had a right to be proud. She was wrong.

"His father is very upset," Eric's mother told Mrs. Fane. "He thinks Eric is abnormal. After all, children are usually more honest in their painting; they are bolder and less inhibited. My husband is a painter, too, you know. A modern. It upsets him that Eric should be so stiff and formal. He is quite disturbed."

Mrs. Fane was even more surprised to learn that Eric's father actually thought the boy was backward because of the way he painted. It had something to do with some subtle principles of art which she didn't quite understand, but at least it gave her a chance to find out what was bothering Eric. She asked a lot of questions and learned that Eric was having a very hard time at home. Jane was the favorite. Father loved her, Mother loved her, and Harold loved her. Eric did, too, but he wasn't as demonstrative as Harold. Mrs. Fane got the impression that in that family one either loved Jane or else.

Harold was jealous of Eric when he was born: he began to wet his bed again, although he had stopped that practice two years before; he had nightmares; he demanded attention; and once he lifted the two-month-old Eric out of his crib and hid him in a closet. Of course, Eric cried and he was quickly rescued. Harold was punished and warned that he had to love Eric; eventually he did. At least, Harold made noises which his family interpreted as love for his little brother and he took Eric as his responsibility. The parents, you see, were compounding their errors: Harold should have been permitted to be jealous; they should have known that he couldn't help being jealous and that he couldn't help showing it. Ideally, he should have been loved more to make Eric seem less of a threat to him. Failing that, he should never have been punished for his honest (and understandable) expression of his feelings.

By this time the reader knows, I trust, that a child can be "normal" and still fail to love his brothers and sisters, that he should be permitted, in fact, to hate them, and that this isn't necessarily a sign of permanent viciousness in the child. But Harold's parents felt that their son should love his brother, even if he had to be forced to do so, and at the cost of burying his resentment. He laid away his hatred where his parents couldn't see it: in the back of his mind, and he showed on the surface what his family thought was love. He got approval for "loving" Eric; it was more comfortable and in every way more desirable than the punishment which was sure to follow any display of jealousy. He took care of Eric: he watched him, played with him, helped him; and Eric adored him. Yet, in the back of his mind, there was always that resentment which needed some way of expressing itself; eventually it was expressed, but in a way which wasn't easily recognized by Harold, Eric, or their parents. That, as you remember, happens to be the way unconscious resentment acts: it is seldom, if ever, revealed for what it is.

Harold never again openly showed his resentment of Eric's favored place in their parents' affection. That it was there was shown when Jane was born: he was able to give up Eric and concentrate on the new baby. Also, he got approval for this, too. His parents loved Jane, didn't they? And didn't they shy away from Eric? Harold could have shown that he had no choice but to drop Eric and adopt Jane. They punished him the last time he didn't love a new baby, when Eric was born. His reaction was accepted by the family, and no one suspected that in addition to getting their approval for being a good boy, Harold was also getting even with Eric. Most of this Mrs. Fane deduced from her interview with the mother.

"You should have seen the way Harold behaved when I brought Jane home from the hospital," she said. "He jumped up and down and was *so* delighted. Eric was keeping in the background but Harold made a point of taking him over to the baby and saying, 'Look Eric! Look how darling she is! Isn't she the cutest ever? Gee, I *love* her!' "

One can imagine what happened that day and the days that followed: Eric somewhat dazed by the loss of attention—to him, a sudden, tearing loss of love—and awed by the prestige of the baby girl. Everybody loved her, including Harold whom Eric adored, and his parents who once loved him. There was a question he had to ask himself: "Why do they love her more than they love me?" This is the question all children ask themselves, and you can be sure that almost always the answer is in some way self-derogatory and self-accusatory. Eric was no different in his approach to the answer, but he also thought up a solution: they loved her more because she was a girl. "Perhaps," he may have decided, "if I were a girl they'd love me, too." So he handed in his resignation from boyhood and withdrew from virtually all boylike activities.

Mrs. Fane found out that the parents made no bones about Jane's being their favorite. "How could you help it?" the mother asked. "You've seen her. She's a real person, talented, charming—a seductress. My husband adores her so— Frankly, I wonder sometimes that I'm not jealous of her; I don't stand a ghost of a chance with her in the running."

The situation, Mrs. Fane thought, called for a psychiatrist, but she didn't think Eric's family would agree. She had a few long talks with Eric's mother, and explained that the boy could well become a homosexual because of his present behavior. Eric wanted to be a girl because, obviously, everybody loved girls more than they loved boys: his father and mother did, and so did Harold. It would be necessary to love Eric more and Jane less for a while, probably for a long time, and his father would have to join the campaign, too. Also, no more wearing Harold's old clothes; the family could afford to buy him his own things. And Eric should be praised and given more approval for his paintings, even if they offended his father's artistic sense. There was plenty of time for him to develop taste; right now, as a child, he needed a sense of being important in his own right more than anything else. He wasn't to be discouraged for his effeminate pursuits, but no one should encourage him to cook or sew. Mrs. Fane had more to say and a lot of explaining to do.   •

Eric did fine, but it took a long time. In a few months there were some very pronounced changes, and at the end of a year he was up to his class in reading. Mrs. Fane got one very aggressive boy to play with him, and Eric's mother often invited this boy to the house. Eric became outspoken for the first time, and gradually he could take his place in the boys' games with naturalness and a slight degree of success. He began to paint in school—he was easily the best—and this helped him build up his confidence in himself. Mrs. Fane thought that Eric's rebellion against modern art was really a rebellion against his father, who failed to love him. Time will tell. All we know is that Eric is now apparently a normal-acting boy.

It's dangerous to acknowledge openly that one child is the favorite in a family. The favored one gets more approval and is made to feel more secure, but when parents pick out one child for praise and adoration they make the other children feel unloved, unprotected, and therefore insecure. Harold had learned his lesson: his wasn't the answer to the problem of making a child feel more secure, because there is still the possibility that he may continue to need outlets for his unconscious resentment of his younger brother. Nor should we overlook another possible source of resentment: Jane. His exuberant acceptance of her was a way of getting his parents' approval, at the same time that he got revenge on Eric. And Eric's insecurity grew by leaps and bounds because his whole family made Jane the favorite.

Parents should avoid favoritism and they should be aware that it affects *all* the children, and not just the favorite child. There is, as I have tried to show, great danger to the middle child, caught between a jealous older child and a favored younger one; parents should always be on the lookout for such situations. It's hard to do anything about it sometimes, but occasionally just knowing what's going on may serve to change the parents' attitudes toward the children, and for the better.

For instance, Mrs. Tilton was aware that her second child,

Danny, was jealous of the baby, Mackie. Danny couldn't make up his mind whether or not to go to camp that first summer, when he was seven. He had always wanted to, because his older brother went, but here he was wavering and changing his mind. No one was forcing him to go (Mrs. Tilton wouldn't have minded his staying in town) and when the school director, who ran the camp, asked her if she knew why Danny was so very uncertain, Mrs. Tilton said: "He told me that he thought Mackie would be sitting in my lap all summer. I don't know what to do." Miss Link, the school director, told her to get Danny to call her when he made up his mind. Danny called her and finally decided once more that he would go. Miss Link told him that this was his last chance to change his mind, because the trunks would be gone in a few days, and then it would be too late.

Danny went, but wouldn't eat. Miss Link knew what was wrong, so his older brother, Kerry, was told to sleep in the same cottage with him. Danny's appetite returned and he seemed to be doing fine. Parents' Day came and Mrs. Tilton arrived for a visit. Danny was perfect all day, except that when his mother was leaving he threw a temper tantrum. Mrs. Tilton asked Miss Link's advice again. It was decided that Mrs. Tilton would stay overnight and see Danny for a long talk the next morning. She didn't need the talk: the next morning Danny was playing baseball and could barely spare a moment to kiss his mother good-by.

All he needed to reassure him was to know that she would, in a pinch, love him. Children can adjust to almost any situation if they know that their parents love them; insecurity means doubts: the child is afraid that the other children are loved more, and that means that he is loved less. No child wants to be loved less: he wants what the others have and it's up to his parents to supply it, or else give him a reasonably accurate facsimile.

The middle child doesn't always give up the fight and become submissive. He has other choices: he can fight back and demand his rights, or he can try to make up for the neglect he suffers at home by becoming completely independent. As an example of this, let's examine the story of Jim Fuller. He has an older brother, Bert, and a younger sister; they're all grown up now.

Bert, the oldest, was slow learning to walk and talk. As he grew older he didn't co-ordinate well; when he was with children his own age he was shy and couldn't hold his own. His parents realized that he needed extra care, so they gave it to him. The second child, Jim, was the exact opposite of his brother. He was strong, healthy, and quick—able to hold his own in any group. The baby, Sally, was a very happy child, the delight of her brothers.

Jim grew up knowing that Bert's slowness meant that he needed special attention and care; outwardly at least Jim seemed to accept this. Sometimes the brothers would quarrel, but Bert was always protected by his parents because he was the weaker of the two. You can sympathize with them: they were trying to turn Bert into a normal child by building up his self-esteem.

Jim became more and more independent; if he wanted attention he didn't show it. He was never the kind of child who seemed to need cuddling or physical contact. In high school he was known as "The Lone Wolf" because he didn't attach himself to any special friends or groups. Two things are significant: he was and still is a nail biter, and he wet his bed until he was about eleven.

He is now being psychoanalyzed and he is beginning to discover all the pent-up resentment he felt when he was younger. He is a charming young man, witty and well-informed, but is still the Lone Wolf. It's as if he were still saying: "I don't need anybody's help." Some people think he is ungenerous and hard-boiled, but he isn't; occasionally you catch a glimpse of the little boy who is grateful for attention that he doesn't expect. When he was a child he had to cover up his real feelings; his childhood needs were repressed. His reaction then became a mixture of bravado and disinterest which fooled everybody, including himself.

That's why it's a good idea to know that a child may be jealous even though he doesn't show it. Parents should try to let the child know that they love him in spite of his seeming indifference. He may not seem to want physical demonstrations of love, but there are other ways of making a contact with him. Sometimes he can be reached through his hobbies: getting him extra supplies for his collections—whatever they may be—will flatter him because he will know his parents are interested in him. We get along better with other adults when we talk to them about their pet subjects, and it works with children, too. Taking him on trips, or giving him special privileges, will do wonders.

After all, what we are trying to do is to keep him from being alone with his grief and his worries—that's a burden too heavy for him to handle by himself. His family should be something he can depend upon when he needs it; all of us need some reassurance that someone loves us. When we get it, we don't need to be Lone Wolves or hard-boiled to cover up our loneliness.

With the middle child one more point is important. Very often, with our small families of today, the third child is the last. A mother who knows this may be more intense about the baby and its arrival than she was about the birth of the other two. She will probably enjoy baby tending, this being the last time, and she will expect the oldest child to take care of the second. There is no reason why the baby shouldn't be satisfying, and the routine less of a nuisance than it seemed before. But the second child will have to develop some mechanism for coping with his jealousy without hurting the older brother, whom he admires, or the baby, whom everyone seems to admire. Usually he hurts himself. He should be watched for silent withdrawal, or any other change in his ordinary behavior, and then reassured. There is this to be remembered about the middle child of three: he may think that four people are against him. The older child and the younger child may actually be so; unless his parents do something about it, he'll think they are in on the plot, too.

CHAPTER X

When the Children's Ages
Are Close Together

———

JEALOUSY will appear in children born two years apart as frequently as in children ten years apart; one won't avoid jealousy by "spacing" children close together or years apart. But we do know that it will become more complicated when the child cannot or will not express his feelings; this will happen when he is too young to be able to say he is jealous, or when his parents won't permit him to express his feelings.

The child who is two years old or less when the baby is born can't come right out and say, "Want to know something? I don't like your brat; I'm jealous of her." But his actions are clear enough: he has begun to soil himself, he is more demanding, and he's awake at the most inconvenient hours. It's up to his parents to interpret his behavior and to understand that he means he is jealous. In Chapter I, I told you about Georgiana and her brother Johnny, whose parents refused to believe that there was any jealousy between them. Georgiana, if you remember, is less than a year older than Johnny; she takes his toys away from him, refuses to share her own toys with him, blithely knocks him down when he is in her way, and does whatever she can to show her parents that she resents her brother, that she is jealous of him. Her parents once told me that they know her like a book, but their insistence that she "love" Johnny is dangerous play. She doesn't love Johnny; she shouldn't have to, as a matter of fact—not at her age, anyway. There is plenty of time for the two children to grow to like each other, once they get over the feeling that each is a threat to the other child. For the present, all that is happening is that Georgiana is forced, against her will, to make believe she loves her brother. She hates him, really, but she can get parental approval by putting on an act—or she can get punishment for acting out her real feelings.

On the other hand, there could be real dangers in such situations, if the child acts out *all* of his resentment against his rival. Suppose, for example, Georgiana decides to clout Johnny on the head with one of his heavier toys. This is a decision which, although natural and honest, she must never be permitted to carry out, not only for the sake of Johnny's continued physical well-being, but also for Georgiana's peace of mind. The child who commits a vicious act soon becomes convinced that he can do only vicious things. I have already mentioned that parents have to step in and stop their children from being bad. Children *want* to be good; they can't help themselves when they show tendencies to be bad, as when they have sudden outbursts of temper; they appreciate, more than parents realize, their parents' efforts to stop them from their own vicious impulses.

Remember, too, that punishment, *after* an attack has been carried out, is useless and harmful: it helps to convince the child that he has been bad. The answer is that parents have to be continually on the watch; they have to be able to step in just as the child is about to express his feelings by an act of mayhem. Parents who cannot take the time, or don't have the time, to be around their children when they play (and perhaps fight) together excuse their own negligence by concluding that their child is vicious, that he has homicidal instincts, and that, as happens in far too many cases, it will have to be beaten out of him.

All children are known to react this way to their own misbehavior. They don't have to know right from wrong in the sense that adults use the terms: to a child, right is what gets him approval; wrong is associated with punishment. That's why the feelings of self-condemnation can start very early in life and show up more quickly among children whose ages are close together. For one thing, these children are very young when jealousy hits them: they react spontaneously and roughly; older children restrain themselves because they are more familiar with the ways of avoiding loss of approval.

A two-year-old child in a nursery group will hit another child with a block, or throw something, without any idea of hurting anybody. He doesn't know that it will hurt. With or without jealousy you have to watch for the unpremeditated attack when there are very young children around. Nursery teachers know this well; they are gentle and patient, but always alert. When a child makes a gesture of biting or hitting another child, the teacher directs the aggressor gently and firmly into another activity.

She may get him to pound pegs with a hammer just to release his feelings. She may say, "We don't hit people, Tommy. Could you build with the blocks? I'll help you." And she does help him: she takes his hand, gets out the blocks or the pegboard, or gets him some clay which he can pound. Then she sits with him for a while. When one child constantly hits or bites, another teacher is assigned to watch him carefully: he is diverted, picked up if necessary, and shown a lot of attention. At nap time the teacher sits with him and rubs his back or talks softly to him. She never says: "You are naughty. Bad boy!"

You might think that this rewards the child who attacks others. It isn't quite that. The teacher is showing him, first of all, that he is a nice boy but needs help in managing himself. She is also showing him how he can get satisfaction from less aggressive activities and she is saving him from the results of his own destructive impulses. Parents visiting a nursery school are sometimes amazed at the change in their little two-year-olds in the playroom. A child who breaks his toys at home will often spend a morning putting wooden trains together. He feels protected: no other child will pull his toy away. If anyone does, he knows that the teacher will get it back for him.

There is another difficulty when the children are both very young which is almost too obvious to mention. We have spoken about handling the problem of jealousy in children by letting them—even encouraging them to—talk it out. Well, try that sometime on a fourteen-month-old baby.

On the other hand, there are some advantages in having children around when they are about the same age. It's hard to give enough affection to all of them so that none feels slighted, but that should be the goal of parents who want to avoid serious problems with jealousy. When the children are born a year or so apart it's easier than when they are four to eight years apart. The reason? For one thing, two children born so close together are infants at virtually the same time; both are quite helpless, and both need much the same kind of care. Since neither has extra benefits, the problem of jealousy is more easily avoided. As I will explain in greater detail in the next chapter, the five-year-old child may be up against two things: one, he may have been the *only* child in the family for five years, with all the privileges and rights of the only child; two, his mother may have had no baby to play with for some time: her excessive enthusiasm could easily be an unpleasant shock to the older child.

As a most natural matter of fact, children who are born close together can so easily share the same amount of love from their parents—who are most likely to give them both the same amount of love—that the question of jealousy can be disregarded the first days with the new baby. For one thing, the one-year-old child is too small to understand and wouldn't know what he was being told or what his parents were trying to do.

These children can't express their feelings in words but sometimes they express even jealousy in other ways. It's surprising how so many so-called sickly babies are suddenly better after getting a full dose of parental affection, especially the maternal type of affection, applied as frequently as possible. If that's the cure, couldn't it be assumed that some part of the frequent colds, middle-ear infections, and stomach disorders, are caused by a lack of that affection? Sometimes, unfortunately, the mother is impatient and neglects the child because he has been troublesome and bothersome. And sometimes the neglect appears to be unavoidable, because the mother is simply unable to take care of two infants at the same time. Whatever the reason, the results are almost always the same: the feelings of jealousy are repressed, and the child will show more obvious symptoms later in life.

Even when the older child is eighteen months or so of age it's hard to explain to him that his hateful feelings toward the baby are justifiable, that he has a right to be jealous—which is the accepted formula for handling jealousy, you remember. Any child is in serious trouble if he isn't permitted to express himself honestly and openly about how he feels. The child of fourteen who isn't permitted to express his jealousy of his little sister is in exactly the same boat as the child of two who is forced to love her baby brother.

Probably the closest one will ever come to a single answer to the problem of jealousy in children is in knowing that it's far healthier for a child to allow him to be jealous than to suppress it. You are forcing him to hate himself because he's unable to suppress such an undesirable—to his parents—emotion. Also, I must mention again that it is utterly useless to try to force children to love each other when they are jealous of each other: parents who think they have jealousy under control will be most unhappy to learn that it is more likely to be under cover, buried in the child's unconscious. Emotional maturity among brothers and sisters is a matter of their mutual love and respect, of genuine friendliness and affection for each other. It isn't just a superficial thing: when this feeling isn't genuine, you can be sure that the child may become excessively competitive. Rivalry, hatred, and jealousy of others outside of his family appear later in life: unconsciously he is trying to make up for his failure to be better than, or as good as, his own brothers and sisters.

There are many ways of fostering jealousy between children who are almost the same age, but most of the opportunities occur later on in life. Children should not be compared to each other. This is a bad practice in any family, but it is more impressive and easier to do when the children are twins or when they are a year or so apart in age. Sometimes the children are close rivals at school, with the younger one resenting the older one's being just a grade or a year ahead of him, and the older one trying to hold on to his advantage as a matter of self-protection. At home there are more difficulties: the children are given similar household duties, and it's easy to compare their efficiency or their co-operation.

When the children are about the same size there is the temptation to save the older child's clothing for the younger one to wear. Girls resent wearing their older sisters' clothing and boys resent wearing their older brothers' clothing. Girls have a better excuse: styles change quickly, and last year's dresses are no longer being worn by the other girls in high school. It isn't only fashion: it is resentment that the older child has more advantages. Boys will express just as much resentment, with less reason to complain of a change in style.

The case of the Manton family shows a number of things parents can overlook when they are bringing up children who are about the same age. There were four children here, two girls and two boys; there was five years difference between the oldest and the youngest. When Ada was thirty-two, Fred thirty-one, Herbert thirty, and Rhoda twenty-eight, the three oldest had been or were being psychoanalyzed; Rhoda was not, but because of the trouble she is having with one of her children she has had a number of interviews with the child's psychiatrist.

When two or more children in a family are psychoanalyzed, it isn't because they have the same disease (they may have) but usually because they have the same parents. Mr. and Mrs. Manton were married when they were in their early thirties, and they wanted to have as many children as they possibly could before, as they put it, "we got too old to appreciate them." Offhand I would say this is a good idea: parents who are too old for their children are never able to treat them as contemporaries; to their too old parents, the children will always be much too young. That's what happens when a grandmother brings up a child, too. From the purely physical point of view, one should know that it becomes increasingly difficult for a woman to have babies when she is nearing forty, unless she has had them earlier, too. As far as the children are concerned, there may be too many of them all around the same age for them to be cared for properly. The Mantons were professional people. Both were successful lawyers and fairly well established before they decided to get married and have children.

I have before me the records in the Manton case. They were given me by four of my colleagues. Each had seen one of the Manton children. Ada, the oldest, told her doctor that she needed help because she was having a terrible time just living. She was a very unhappy person: she couldn't stand people, couldn't be alone, couldn't ride in taxis, busses, or trains, couldn't walk in the street, and couldn't sit still at home, either. She was unhappily married and worried about it; she had no children.

When he first saw her, her doctor was impressed with her childlike voice and appearance: she used lipstick but no other make-up, and she wore attractive clothes which were obviously bought in the young misses' and teen-age shops. She had the figure for it, small and slight, and she had the gestures for it, and a plaintive, childlike voice, which gave people the impression that she was in her early twenties rather than in her early thirties.

"That's one of the things I came to see you about," she told her doctor. "I lie about my age to everyone. I can't stand being thirty-two and I can't stand being married."

He asked her if it was just recently that she began to lie about her age, and she said, "Well, not very recently. It started six years ago, when Rhoda got married."

"How old was Rhoda when she got married?" he asked.

"She was twenty-two. I was almost twenty-seven when that happened," she said, and her voice was almost bitter. "But I don't want you to think that I resented it."

"Why didn't you resent it?" he asked her. "Were you about to be married, too?"

"No, not then," she said. "I was very happy for her. I love her dearly; in fact, we all love each other in the family dearly."

"Let's put it this way," he said. "Didn't you even resent the fact that her marriage made you change your age?"

"I'll tell you what I resented," she said, bitterly and angrily. "I resented everybody looking at me as if it was a shame that she got married first. I resented the way my brothers began to take me out, to keep me happy, so I wouldn't miss not having a boy friend. I resented the fact that Rhoda always got the best of everything, and that when I came home with a boy friend Rhoda would take him over. She did that from the time she was sixteen. I resented the fact that Rhoda didn't even have to go to college, or study anything, or have a career."

She had never thought of her sister in these terms before, as it turned out. Nor had she ever thought of herself as someone who was jealous, because in her family one just was never jealous of anyone else.

"We were a closely knit group," she said, "and we were taught to love each other, from as far back as I can remember. It shocks me to think that I could have been so resentful of Rhoda's good luck. I never felt that way before and I don't believe I feel that way now—it's just that I got upset when you suggested that I might resent her. No, I don't resent her. I love her, I love her husband and her children. The kids are crazy about me. Sometimes I get a little embarrassed to go out to visit Rhoda, because the kids are so fond of me. Like last week, when I took them for a ride in the car. I feel terrible about it now, because the little boy—his name is Arthur —he has a cold; I guess it's because he didn't wear a coat and I had the top down. I suppose you'll say it was done on purpose, because I hate children and resent Rhoda's happiness."

It was quite possible that she left the top of the car down unconsciously, because of her unconscious resentment of her sister and her sister's good fortune. Consciously she could not remember that she was ever jealous of her brothers and her sister. Later in her analysis she dimly recalled that her mother used to say she had been a very sick baby, that it began when Fred was born, and that she required a good deal of attention. Her mother also remarked that Ada seemed to get sick again each time another baby arrived. "It was almost as if you didn't like the baby to get all the attention," her mother said. She remembered, too, that when Herbert, the second brother, wanted to have a bicycle like Fred's—Herbert was only eight at the time—he carried on and cried and said, "I hate you all!" She remembered this because it was the only time there was ever any expression of less than love among the four children. She also remembered that her mother told Herbert that he must never be jealous of his brother or his sisters, that the only way in which the Manton family would live was by loving each other; as far as she knew, Herbert never hated anyone in the family again.

There was intense rivalry among the three older children in school and at home; Rhoda was really outside of the clique formed by the three older children, so she wasn't a rival of theirs. She suffered the usual fate of the youngest child: she grew up to be extremely immature. When she said she didn't want to go to college the family breathed a sigh of relief. Everyone agreed that she would never be as smart in school as the three older children. She had never made as good marks as they did in grammar school and in high school, and they were quite sure she could never stand the pace in college.

All this was entirely unfair to Rhoda; she was as intelligent as the other children, but she never had a chance to show it. As time went on she, too, was convinced she wasn't intelligent. The reason, of course, was the rivalry of the three older children, which was fostered and encouraged by the parents. From the time they started in school, Ada, Fred, and Herbert were each trying to gain their parents' approval by being brighter than the others. They raised each other's standards by studying hard and, as a result, were far better than their classmates. They had more incentive, while Rhoda had none at all: all that was required of her was that she remain a baby. In this the children fell in with their mother's plan: having waited so long for babies, Mrs. Manton wanted to prolong the pleasure of having one for as long as possible; Rhoda was the natural victim, and stayed a baby for too long a time. It's no wonder that Rhoda, pigeonholed by her family as the baby, grew up convinced of her inability and inadequacy as a person.

Another interesting development took place in this family in the way the children lined up. As I pointed out in Chapter IX, the middle child is apt to get it from both ends, the oldest child and the youngest ganging up on him. Thus, Ada should have been most fond of Herbert, with Fred as their victim. With a fourth child present, Fred should have adopted her as his ally for protection against Ada and Herbert. Part of this did happen: Ada found Fred a little too close for comfort, in school, at play, and at home. She was the oldest, and should have been the leader of the family, but Fred was. His parents gave him some of those male privileges which even an oldest daughter doesn't have, and he was pretty well entrenched as a definite threat to Ada. She turned her back on Fred as if to say: "He won't bother me if I don't know he's there," and courted Herbert. It was as obvious as this: when she was in the third grade and Fred in the second, she never missed an opportunity to ignore his pleas for help; her excuse was that she had to look after Herbert, who was then in the first grade. She had two motives: she wanted Fred to fail, so that she could maintain her supremacy, and she thought Herbert would look fine on her team, to give her what help she might need against Fred. (Remember that these were not at all conscious motives; the Mantons were not supposed to hate each other or to be jealous—openly.)

I might point out that the division of brothers and sisters

in a family isn't always a matter of two against the middle child: complications set in when the battle is between sexes. Ada Manton found herself deserted by Herbert when he and Fred went off to play; she fixed herself on Rhoda as a last, desperate, but highly satisfactory, resort. There were more motives that made this move appear to be advisable: first, two girls against two boys seemed safer; second, it would enhance her position with her parents if she were attentive to the baby, their favorite; third, it might help her to compensate for her feeling of being rejected by Herbert. This wasn't the first time she had felt rejected: one wonders whether the reason she was a sickly child—especially when the other children were born—was because of feeling rejected by her parents. Also, this wasn't the last time she was going to feel rejected: the next time was when Rhoda ran out on her.

The way this happened was logical enough. Rhoda found out, as she grew older, that the boys were her chief competitors, so she joined forces with them. They couldn't keep her away because she was their parents' favorite; also, to their amazement and occasional horror, the other boys thought she was cute and pretty, and liked her, so she stayed. Also, there is reason to believe that Fred was happy in this arrangement, which was the pattern of two against the middle child. He resented Herbert, who was a threat to him, and would naturally have allied himself with Rhoda had not the division of boys versus girls taken place. Consciously—openly—he welcomed Herbert, but unconsciously there was deep resentment, as we shall see later. Rhoda was now in the middle of a well-developed habit of being dependent: on her parents, on Ada, and on both her brothers, especially Fred. Ada, on the other hand, developed the habit of feeling rejected by the same people, so she took to her bed.

It seems that there are just two ways for children to act who are born into a world which to them is very cruel and not at all helpful: they either retire from the battle and are as inconspicuous and docile as possible, or they fight it out, against all odds. Ada and Herbert decided at some point in their lives not to fight; Fred and Rhoda took an aggressive stand. Ada was always sick, the result of her decision not to fight. She grew up with a "cardiac neurosis": a neurosis in which the patient believes that there is something wrong with his heart. Such a person becomes very conscious of his heartbeats, will take his pulse frequently, and will overemphasize any change in speed of the heartbeats, which are normal; he will even have imaginary heart attacks. Ada developed a "heart condition" when she was eleven, for no known medical reason. She stayed home, never went in for any strenuous activities, and let the others take over. Rhoda was a better swimmer and tennis player than she, a better dancer, healthier, taller, and better-looking.

It was very obvious that her so-called heart trouble was the result of a number of psychological factors, not the least of which was her need to be taken care of, as only a child who is sick can be taken care of. Sickness seems to solve so many difficulties, especially when children are having trouble with the other children in the family, as when the others are receiving more attention. To lie in bed, to be waited upon, to be humored, and to have her own way was very attractive to Ada; besides, it helped to convince her that she was forgiven her bad behavior. What bad behavior? There had been no hint, in her interviews with her doctor, that she was feeling guilty about anything in her past, until there came a period where she said less and less about herself. There was something she wasn't willing to talk about, something that had been preying on her mind.

Some patients can't speak frankly and openly about themselves while they are in analysis, which is the one place in the world they are expected to. When this happens, the analysis seems to bog down. Then the patient may reveal something that has bothered him for years, something he's terribly ashamed of. The trouble is often sexual, but it can be guilt about stealing, lying, copying in school, and other things. Ada's trouble was sexual.

The story she told was this: when she was twelve years old,

Fred, aged eleven, seduced her. Mrs. Manton had gone back to active law practice with her husband when Rhoda was about four years old. The children were alone in their rooms for long periods of time—the maids and cook were usually busy somewhere else—so they had complete privacy. Fred was bigger than she, Ada said, and she remembered, too, that he made some threat against her, something he would do to her if she told. She said that it was a horrifying experience; Fred had actually had intercourse with her. She was terribly ashamed of what happened, and when she told the story she very hurriedly said: "I guess that's enough damage to a child to make her afraid ever to have anything to do with men again, isn't it?" If that were true there would be a large number of women now happily married who have no reason to be. They are not deprived of a pleasurable sex life just because, as children, they indulged in sexual play with their brothers, or with other boys. Psychiatrists know that children who play sexually are indulging their curiosity rather than their viciousness. However, they will be convinced that they are vicious when they are told they are by older people. Thus feelings of guilt come upon the children and stay with them.

Ada seemed to be somewhat relieved when she learned that what she had done was not the most horrible example of sexual perversion her doctor ever heard of, because then she told him that she had had the same experience with Herbert; she was "not sure" if she had made the advances or if Herbert had. She and Herbert had continued the practice for a number of months and then stopped.

The damage had been done before the children even tried to play at their sexual games: they had been told that masturbation was wicked, and they would associate masturbation—and guilt—with anything that had to do with their genital organs. Ada's guilt was worse because she was the oldest and she should have known better. She had been told this by her mother for so many years she began to believe it herself. She didn't have to seduce her brothers in order to feel that she was the most wicked of the three: all she had to do was participate in the act; her feeling that she wasn't as good as her brothers did the rest.

Ada was in love with her husband, with whom she acted even younger than she made herself appear to be. But she couldn't let him touch her; she was terribly frightened when they went to bed. And yet her fantasies when she masturbated (for she continued to masturbate) were about lurid orgies. It was obvious from the start that she thought herself a debased person, capable of the wildest sexual acts.

Her marriage was unsuccessful because she tried so hard to forget her sins by remaining immature—even infantile. She seemed to wish that she were a child; if she were one she would be younger than Rhoda, who was now a mother. "Younger than Rhoda"—that meant that *she* would be the baby of the family. Sexual intercourse was grown-up; she shunned it. In addition, she was afraid of her own passion. "I seem to be afraid that if I give in, if I let myself go, that I would be capable of almost anything, and it's so shameful." To avoid having intercourse with her husband too frequently she used the excuse that her heart was bad and that she had to avoid strenuous activity.

The story of Fred was very interesting. He was competitive in his own family circle—he was one of those who fight the hostility around them—and his aggressiveness and competitiveness showed in his desire to be the best in everything. Deep down inside he felt inadequate—because he felt he had failed to get his parents' love away from Ada, Herbert, and Rhoda. He would have to be the best to prove to everyone that he was *not* inadequate. He was jealous of his sisters and he felt that they were the cause of his troubles. He had sexual relationships with his sister to prove that he was superior to her, knowing that she would be shamed by what he had done to her. When he grew up his attitude toward women was the same: a woman was only of importance to him if he could be cruel to her; he was sadistic in his sexual experiences. Fred resented Ada's advantages as the oldest one in the family; later he resented her taking up with Herbert. Of course, his alliance with Herbert against the girls showed that he needed more ways to prove he was superior to Ada. In addition, by involving her in a sexual escapade he may have been expressing his unconscious jealousy of her. He had always thought he was evil and wicked because he masturbated, and his wickedness made him inferior to Ada. Also, being wicked seemed to explain why Ada and Rhoda were preferred to him. Ada was not evil, she was good, and it suited his purposes to have her be declared—in his mind, at least—evil, too.

Fred's jealousy of Ada made him very competitive with her: he wasn't content just to equal her grades, and he tried to exceed her. He was abetted when his parents compared his grades to Ada's: when he got better grades she would become discouraged and give up.

He was jealous of his brother Herbert, too, but here he had much less competition. He took over Herbert's education. His parents expected him to do it and encouraged him. As a result, Herbert was completely under Fred's influence. He did what Fred told him. He had periods when he was convinced he was worthless only because Fred had said he was. In this, he reacted very much the way Ada had: he became docile and he gave up his fight against the world. Herbert had a good chance to become a fine pianist, but Fred insisted that he learn how to play baseball, too. Fred had no musical ability whatsoever, but he was such a fine teacher of baseball that Herbert made the high-school baseball team when he was thirteen, as catcher; Fred, of course, was the pitcher. The result was that Herbert had three fingers on his left hand smashed, which ruined his piano playing for good. Fred had not consciously wanted anything of the sort to happen, but unconsciously he may have.

Rhoda was compared to Ada in ways that made her only too well aware and too envious of her younger sister's beaux and good looks. On the other hand, Herbert and Fred were compared in a much more harmful way: they were made conscious of the size of their genital organs, to Herbert's everlasting detriment. He was one of those children who are born

with undescended testicles, a condition which can be cor-
rected with an operation; he was operated on when he was
nine years old. By that time he had been told a number of
times by his parents, and he could see for himself, that his
genital organs were not as large as Fred's. Once or twice—he
thought it was accidental and innocent—his mother mentioned it, once on the occasion of her purchasing bathing
trunks for Fred, Herbert, and Mr. Manton. Herbert was
rather tall, almost as tall as his father. When he tried on the
trunks his mother said, "I think you'd better give those to
your father. He has more there than you have, and his trunks
are a little tight for him."

Herbert became a homosexual. He told his analyst that he
had tried to have sexual relations with girls but had failed;
his feelings of guilt about his sister seemed to keep him from
going out with girls. He wanted to get married and even
wanted to have children, but he was afraid that his homosexuality would impel him to leave his wife and go out with
other men. He had a girl, but he was not interested in her
sexually. A doctor had suggested that he have a spermatozoa
test made; it's possible that boys with undescended testicles
remain sterile for the rest of their lives if the operation is not
performed early enough. When the laboratory report came
back it was very discouraging: it showed that there were some
normal spermatozoa present, but these were few in number
and so outnumbered by abnormal forms that the laboratory
technician wrote: "To all intents and purposes this can be
considered sterile semen."

During the course of Herbert's psychoanalysis it became
evident that he felt he was inadequate in everything, especially inadequate as a man. He was a dependent person: he
had never been dependent enough on his mother. He was
dependent on Ada and then on Fred. As a reaction to his feelings of inadequacy, he needed to prove himself superior to
other men. It became increasingly clear that he was a homosexual because the act itself put him in a position of superiority to another man. "Another man" meant to him all

men, including his brother Fred. He was the passive partner in his homosexual relationships: he never actually made love to his partners, but would let men make love to him.

Probably the most interesting feature of this case was the fact that some two years after his psychoanalysis began, Herbert got married and, because he fully understood why he had been a homosexual, had no trouble whatsoever in his marital relations. Perhaps that's an understatement: he and his wife are the parents of a baby girl, despite the pessimistic laboratory report. It happens sometimes that unconscious psychological factors produce impotence or sterility, just as they can produce other bodily ailments. Psychotherapy, in many cases, removes the psychological cause and there is normal functioning again.

Herbert's jealousy of Fred was another result of the odious comparisons made by their parents: he was inferior sexually, mentally, and socially. He was not allowed to make friends of his own, especially of his own age, and had to go out with older boys, Fred's friends.

This is a dangerous procedure: younger children should not be forced to accept the friends of their older brothers or sisters. It may impose a burden on the older child who has to take care of the kid brother or sister. It also puts the younger child in a very unfavorable position, because he can hardly hope to compete physically (and sometimes mentally) with the older boys. Fred, being an aggressive and competitive person, was able to make friends two or three years older than himself; he could meet them and beat them on their terms. Taking Herbert into this group only emphasized his inadequacies. Jealousy occurs more frequently in those who are less competent; it's too obvious that they aren't as good as their rivals. When they are in competition and fail, it increases their resentment of the others.

Rhoda suffered the fate of many children who are the youngest in the family: she was pampered, forgiven, petted, made too much of, excused from irksome duties, and got everything she asked for. The result was that she never had the slightest inkling of how to accept responsibilities. Everything was done for her and she came to expect this for the rest of her life. She didn't have to keep up with the other children in school, and when she wanted to stay home she was allowed to stay home. She was thoroughly spoiled, a willful child, and no restraint was ever placed on her activities. The youngest child, the baby of the family, is jealous of the older children because they are older, bigger, better able to take care of themselves, and they seem to have things that she doesn't have. She can get even with them by taking advantage of her position as the baby of the family; she can make demands on them, be dependent on them, and report them to her parents if they don't do exactly as she says. Rhoda had everyone in her family taking care of her and at her beck and call. It was the only way she could get even with her brothers and sister.

She entered into an early marriage, and seemed to be very well adjusted. But that isn't the whole story. She has had numerous extramarital affairs and is highly dissatisfied in her sexual relations with all men. She is what psychoanalysts refer to as a "frigid" woman, which must seem to the layman an interesting way to describe someone who is promiscuous. The story behind her promiscuity and frigidity is similar to Fred's: ashamed of her early sexual thoughts, she is trying to prove that she was *not* wicked by having as many affairs as she possibly can. At the same time she can't get over her childish feeling that it *is* wicked, so she must not allow herself to enjoy it: she has never been satisfied. And we mustn't overlook her jealousy of Ada; her desire to be as attractive to as many men as possible is another part of the mechanism: she is still trying to be wanted by more men than Ada.

"Imagine what a hectic family life they would have had if those kids had *really* begun to express themselves," I thought I heard you say. I can imagine it: it would have been noisy, painful, and raucous—but healthy. Making the children love each other is like relieving pain in the stomach by taking aspirin; the doctor can't find out where the pain is because he can't tell what organ is hurting. That superficial, enforced love which the Mantons demanded that their children show each other covered up their real feelings of jealousy for each other.

There is no doubt that jealousy played the most important part in creating the problems the Manton children grew up with. Each child's jealousy as a new baby arrived was a normal reaction; these children were no different from any others —they were not born vicious or promiscuous. It was the attitude of their parents toward every normal *childish act* which caused each problem to be magnified, each open expression of defiance or resentment to be sent underground.

From each case history in that family I learned that the Manton parents did not want to gratify their children, but to satisfy their own ambitions. They encouraged their children to compete because they wanted admiration for themselves as parents and professional people. They couldn't allow one single act that would reflect on their thoroughness or efficiency. They had an idea that the neighbors' children were dirty and mischievous and wouldn't allow their children to have them in the house. They didn't really want to enjoy *children;* they wanted to enjoy their own power over children, and the feeling of managerial accomplishment that went with it. You are right in thinking that they were cruel parents, as cruel as if they had abandoned their children completely. Jealousy, in this family, was accentuated at every turn.

I chose this family in order to point out in the aggregate some of the things which occur singly in other families. For one thing, Ada used her illness to get attention. Some parents think that "attention-getting" devices should be overlooked or discouraged. They don't realize that the child wouldn't have to resort to such tricks if the need for attention could be satisfied legitimately—if he *got* attention. It is only when a child cannot get attention or love *in any other way* that he has to use illness as an excuse.

This doesn't mean that the sick child—or any other—should be overprotected. Very often a child who has had a severe illness is coddled too long after he is well. In large families especially this can cause even greater jealousy. The child who is given extra privileges, special foods, who is not allowed to play with the other children because he might hurt himself— even though he has completely recovered—can become the object of resentment and dislike, especially if the others have to protect him, too. He should not be encouraged to think that he is abnormal, weak, incompetent, or in need of special favors. Children don't want to be different unless they intend to use their "differences" as a weapon.

A second point to remember with children who are born close together is this: they will find good company among themselves, but they should not have to depend only on each other for companionship. They should have their own friends, with similar interests and comparable abilities, with whom they can let off steam. In every family the children have their own assigned positions of importance; this is normal and natural. The position of leader and the status of the followers is determined by the age, ability, strength, and popularity of each child; their relationship to each other rarely changes in the family. In order to give the leader a taste of following, and the followers a taste of leadership, they must be allowed to make friends away from the family circle.

The third point is this: Children know only too well their parents' attitudes about sex and sex play. We have a lot of proof that most children experiment sexually among themselves. They may be "playing doctor," or they may just tickle and giggle. Children experimented this way in the past, they do today, and they probably will in the future. It's not vicious, nor wicked, nor at all unusual. And children in the same family, left to their own devices together continually, without the company of other children, may even indulge in excessive sex play.

I don't think one has to investigate every closed door; the children would feel guilty and ashamed, no matter what was said. What I want to emphasize is this: where sibling rivalry and resentment are intense, a child will do anything he can to shame or belittle the other child. The more wicked it may be to adults, the more quickly the child will use it to demean his sister or brother. In the Manton family, sex play, or anything connected with the genitals, was considered dirty, degrading, and bad, so each child used it to dirty, degrade, and "make bad" the other children.

Above all, in any family, parents must learn to take open defiance of their wishes, noisy fighting, and expressions of anger and resentment with equanimity. It is much better that the children join together in an overt declaration of the way they feel about their parents than if they take it out on themselves in some disguised way. The domineering father who intimidates his children should be a thing of the past. You can be fairly certain that Mr. Manton would never stand for disrespect, or an expression like "You're crazy, Daddy" which so many fathers take for granted today. Parents should know that outward respect may cover deeply buried resentment and hostility. Also, they might enjoy the familiarity of being friends with their children rather than being figures of righteousness, or symbols of fear.

If parents are at all aware of their children's feelings, and have kindness, generosity, and common sense to boot, their problems will never reach the proportions they did in the lives of Ada, Fred, Herbert, and Rhoda Manton. It's bad when fathers and mothers don't recognize their own selfishness, when they forget that their responsibilities are primarily toward their children. What happened to the Manton children could have been avoided by a parental willingness to put up with some of the to-be-expected inconveniences of being parents, and by restraining the parental impulse to use the children to satisfy superficial parental needs.

CHAPTER XI

Five Years Apart

———◆———

ALL THE classical reasons for jealousy must be thought of when a child is four or five years old, or older, at the time when a baby brother or sister is born. Again I must emphasize the importance of the parents' attitude. They must be able to tell their child that he can be jealous, so that he can express his feelings when he wants to. The first-born child was an only child for a long time; he enjoyed all the privileges of any only child, and his position in the family was unchallenged for five years. The family is really his kingdom; all of his parents' love, all of their interest in him, are his exclusive property; he has gotten used to these things, and he comes to accept them as a matter of course. You can imagine what a shock it must be when he finds his position—and his security —threatened by his parents' interest in someone else. How can he be expected to welcome the baby with anything resembling open arms?

Jealousy in children born many years apart is more readily recognized because it occurs in a child who is able to express himself clearly on the subject. Also, his resentment *is* greater; he really has more reasons to feel deprived of his parents' love. Fortunately, the child is now old enough to understand when he is told why he is jealous; he can be shown that his parents haven't stopped loving him. This is the child who is very much aware of what is going on; he can tell that there are things he is being deprived of. It's up to his parents to let him show his jealousy by letting him talk about it, or act it out. This is the child who is really helped by being prepared for the new baby, and by assisting in the arrangements for the baby's arrival. As I said in Chapter V, this must be done subtly and without too much emphasis on the baby. Nor must it be made into a chore. He should only be permitted to help when he wants to, without too much urging by his parents and without their offering him rewards. He should want to help because he is interested in helping, because it amuses him, and because he likes it, never because it is a means of getting approval. If the older child is a girl the same principles apply.

Girls usually like babies, just as they like dolls, because they identify with the feminine role—the mother's role. I talked about this process of identification earlier, and I will discuss it more fully in Chapter XIII. Identification is the most important way in which a child learns to be a man or a woman. If a mother enjoys maternity and her job as the protector and comforter of her children, her daughter will find them desirable, too. However, taking care of the baby should not become a chore for a little girl, nor should it shut out other satisfactions of childhood. Her responsibility should be small and she should be allowed to be selfish about her playtime and her fun. Responsibility will come with maturity, so whatever she does for the baby and for her mother now should be spontaneous and enjoyable.

Sometimes it is financially impossible for mothers to have help with their housework, and the older children, especially if they are girls, are expected to take over some of the chores. There are families where all the children help according to their abilities and it doesn't seem to cut down their satisfactions, or make them more jealous of the baby. The children feel free to invite their schoolmates in because they have a real interest in their home and they have status as hosts or hostesses. In such families there is often more fun because schedules are not rigid and overneatness is not stressed; the children's friends are welcome for meals and help in serving and cleaning up. There is danger in exploiting the children, or in giving extra approval and rewards for certain kinds of help. On the other hand, if the parents don't appreciate what the older children do and if they accept it too matter-of-factly, there will be resentment against the unexploited youngest member of the family.

One of my colleagues told me about the following case. A mother was quite perturbed over the revolt staged in her home by her oldest child, a daughter aged nine. She ran away from home; she refused to go to school; she fought with her mother and she even struck her a number of times. There were two other children in the family, a boy who was seven and a two-year-old baby girl. The oldest child in such a family would ordinarily welcome the birth of the baby as an ally against the middle child, in this case the brother. When this doesn't happen it can mean either a good understanding between the two older children, or it can be a warning of a serious maladjustment.

The girl, Dora, was very outspoken about the cause of her difficulties. She resented the fact that she had to take care of the baby and more than that she resented washing the baby's diapers. She had never been called upon to do the family laundry before, but her mother was unable to do it all after she had had the baby.

"It wasn't my idea to have a baby," she said. "I don't see why I have to do all that dirty work, and take care of her, too."

She hadn't been very happy in her family even before the baby was born. The doctor asked her to explain.

"Well, ever since I was little," she told him, "I was jealous of my brother George. It always looked as if he got the best of everything. First I thought that my mother and my father didn't care for me any more because they liked George better, but when I grew up I found out that George was neglected, too. He has to do a lot of the work in the house and so do I, and it never seems as if they like us very much."

"How does George feel about it?" the psychiatrist asked her.

"He doesn't like it, either. He once told me I was getting

the best of it, but it wasn't so. Lots of times he can do things that I'm not allowed to do, and I'm older."

There is little jealousy among children who are neglected by their parents, you will remember. Obviously, as in this case, it's because they have to band together to provide each other company for their mutual misery. Also, this would explain why Dora didn't have to look to the baby as an ally against her brother: they had reached some sort of understanding and considered the baby a threat, not only because of jealousy of the baby, but also because of the added injustice.

"No matter how good I am, I never get anything for it," she told the psychiatrist. "They expect me to do everything, and I have to even if I don't want to. Other girls don't do what I have to do around the house, and they can go out and play, and go to club meetings, and they can even have their friends come over to the house. My mother doesn't like that. She says that a whole bunch of kids running around the house makes the house dirty and besides she can't listen to the radio. And anyway, if the house is dirty, I have to clean it up, so what difference should it make to her?"

"Did you look forward to the baby when you knew it was coming?" asked the psychiatrist.

"Yes, I guess I did," she said. "I even sort of hoped it would be a girl, because then there would be two girls and she'd be on my side, sort of."

"Against George?" the doctor asked.

"I guess so," she said, and laughed.

"Don't you like the baby now?" asked the psychiatrist.

"Gee whiz, you couldn't like anything in that family, the way they treat you. When they give you a present for Christmas, it's something I need anyway, like a coat or a dress or a pair of shoes. Well, gee whiz, that's no present for anybody. What's the good of having a present if you have to work all the time to take care of it? That's what they did with this baby. I thought it would be nice to have a baby in the family, and I even thought I'd like to play with it, so instead they make me work and wash out those dirty diapers, and I hate it. Besides, she makes too much noise and wakes everybody up at night. And then they want me to give her a bottle at night, and I have to go to school the next day."

It was fortunate for Dora, and for her parents, that her feelings were so close to the surface. She expressed them in her revolt, which brought her to the clinic. Once there she was allowed to talk freely about what she disliked and the "cure" was simple.

It was obvious that this girl had put up with a lot from her parents, who were a particularly un-understanding pair of people, and the answer to the problem of her misbehavior was re-education of both mother and father. They were told how she felt, and it was pointed out to them that they were expecting too much from her. Too many parents expect too much from their children and it is a problem in child care. The parents complain that the child can't do something or other which is really beyond the child's abilities. One shouldn't expect young children to be able to show as good judgment as adults, or to know all of the fine differences between right and wrong, or to be able to appreciate the seriousness of life. Those things come later, when they are grown. While they are children they should be permitted to act like children and to disregard the more solemn aspects of living.

There are children who are more submissive than Dora, who will gladly undertake the care of the younger child, and this can be serious. There is no rule which says that parents have to be suspicious of the older child who voluntarily and consistently takes care of a younger child, but it would be wise to look into it. For one thing, it may indicate a desire to obtain more approval from their parents. If Jane takes care of Jill and relieves her mother of a good many responsibilities, Jane will receive her mother's grateful appreciation. The question is: why should Jane want so much approval?

It could be, of course, that Jane is really sincere in her desire to take some of the responsibility off her mother's shoulders, but, on the other hand, it could also be that Jane is jealous of Jill and the way Jill monopolizes her parents' affection. Jane may think that by associating with Jill all the time she will get some of the approval which was intended for Jill, the same way that people like to bask in the reflected glory of famous names and try to associate with famous people all the time. You may find that Jane has become a very submissive person, as a reaction to the harsh world she has been born into; she would rather not fight against what she thinks are impossible odds. In that case Jane would be docile and obedient and give up all of her initiative, as well as any incentive she might have to independent thinking. She would allow others to think for her, as an outgrowth of her submissive obedience to her parents. Taking care of Jill would be the only course open for such a child.

There is still another possibility that should be looked into: perhaps Jane has been unable to make a good adjustment with children her own age. Let's say she is smaller than some of the other girls and that she isn't as good as they are in the games they play. She would then find that it would make her uncomfortable and unhappy to be around these other girls, to be reminded time after time of her own ineptness. Jane would then welcome any excuse to avoid associating with her friends. She might put on an act with them, using the baby as an escape, and say, in an imitation of an envious tone, "Gee, I wish I could play with you, but I have to mind the baby."

If Jane is happy in school, has fun with her friends, admits that babies are cute but can also be noisy and bothersome, and shows the normal boisterous behavior of a seven- or eight-year-old at times, then her help with the baby can be accepted as a good identification and a healthy interest. But if Jane suddenly becomes *too* good, especially at home, if she withdraws from her age-mates, if she lacks interest in other things, then parents should discourage her interest in the baby by giving her a lot of approval for the things she does outside of taking care of it.

The amount of interest shown in the baby depends on the

child's age and maturity. For example, parents will find that a six- or seven-year-old girl will spend long hours playing with the baby, or giving him his bottle. Then suddenly, one or two years later, she can't spare ten minutes to watch him while her mother goes to the grocer's. This is just normal growth and change of interest. To a six-year-old the baby's responses and his small clinging fingers may be a very absorbing novelty; at eight or nine, the game of jump-rope on the playground, or the five-o'clock radio program, is much more fascinating. If taking care of the baby brings on the disapproval of the gang, the child will resent bitterly her parents' attempts to make her a baby sitter. This change is normal; if a girl's devotion to the baby *doesn't* change as she grows and her interests don't expand, there may be a reason to feel that she is covering up her jealousy and resentment.

However, no matter how much, or how little, the older child likes to mind the baby, she should never be given too much responsibility for the baby's physical or psychological care; there are too many things that can happen to a baby for which the older child will take the blame. This was one of the interesting features of the case of a young woman (we will call her Edna) whose dependence on her younger brother, six years younger than she, was so pathological that she couldn't get married, or make any kind of normal adjustment to adult living. Despite the fact that she graduated from college *cum laude,* she was convinced that she was unintelligent and felt that her good grades were "what you might expect if you studied eight hours or more a day."

Edna had had three jobs since leaving college, and in each one she managed to get a salary as high as $7500 a year, yet she felt inadequate in her work. She wasn't very realistic in talking about her inadequacy, considering her salaries and the positions she had held: these seemed to indicate that she was highly thought of. She wasn't fired from any of the jobs, but left because she was afraid that her bosses would get on to her; she was under the impression that she was just about getting by and that they would soon find out how inefficient

she was. She told her doctor that she got her jobs by accident, that there was no real ability involved; she said she
knew many people and that it took a lot of pull.

All of this indicated that she was a person who had absolutely no conception of her true worth and was afraid to make
full use of her capabilities. Her work was in the research
field, and consisted of very careful and meticulous searching
out of facts; she was in charge of a group of assistants who
worked well under her. However, as is typical of such a person, she couldn't take a job which required independent
thinking of her own; she could only carry out projects planned
by others. It was obvious from the first that what she wanted
from her doctor was advice, and that she would make the
most desperate efforts to have him tell her what to do and
what decisions to make. She could never make any decisions
for herself. It was as if she were afraid that if she made a decision and it happened to come out wrong, she would have
no one but herself to blame. A psychoanalyst rarely makes
decisions for his patients, nor does he give advice. Patients
try to get him to do so: if his decisions are wrong, then the
patient can say he's a poor psychoanalyst.

Edna had never had to make decisions for herself, she told
her doctor. After her father died she was always able to go
to her brother, even though he was six years younger. She
looked on him as not only a contemporary, but someone more
mature than she. It was her brother's marriage, about two
months before, which finally made her come to see a psychoanalyst. Obviously she no longer had him to give her advice
and she needed someone to take his place; more than that,
there was a possibility that he had been taking her father's
place. This is seen frequently in girls who become dependent
on an older brother when the father is no longer available,
but it was unusual in a girl who was so much older than her
brother.

In tracing the causes of her inability to adjust, her doctor
got this story. When she was four years old, a baby brother
was born. Her mother took sick when this baby was six

months old, and Edna was detailed to take care of some of
the simpler aspects of baby tending; she was supposed to stay
with the baby when he was in the carriage, run for help if
he cried, and fetch small things that he might need. These
demands on her were amply rewarded and her parents were
very understanding about the sacrifices she was making for
the younger child. In looking back, she found great difficulty
in discussing any of her real feelings toward this baby, but
eventually it came out.

She told the rest of this story with tears in her eyes and a
good deal of self-condemnation. Really she resented being
forced to take the baby out, and her father, she felt, was
much more interested in the baby than in her. She didn't
even have her mother to go to because her mother was an
invalid and was not to be disturbed too frequently. She was
jealous of the privileges that the baby had—the baby slept in
the mother's room—and she was jealous of what appeared to
be her father's neglect of her in favor of the baby. She had
often wished that the baby were dead and she remembered
that she used to think that the baby had something to do
with her mother's illness. Added to this was, of course, the
curtailment of her playing with her friends, so that she was
by herself a good deal of the time. However, there were occasions when she was able to have some neighbor wheel the
baby carriage across the street to a little park where she and
her playmates used to get together before she got this new
and unpleasant job. When this happened, she could play
with the girls and still keep an eye on the baby, but she felt
that this was wrong and, had she been caught, she would have
been punished. One day one of her playmates didn't show
up, and later on that afternoon the mothers of some of the
other children came to the park in what seemed to her to be
mysterious haste and with an element of some foreboding.
None of the girls showed up to play for the rest of the week,
and finally Edna found out why: she and four other little
girls developed whooping cough. Edna was confined to her
home; then, in a few days, her baby brother started to cough

and whoop. Whooping cough in infancy is serious and sometimes fatal. The baby brother died.

Edna was much more upset by the baby's death than were
her parents, or so it seemed to her. It's quite possible that
they were trying to cheer her up by playing down their own
sorrow. Her extreme grief led everyone to exclaim over her
devotedness, which made her even more sorrowful. Edna's
parents didn't understand that she was blaming herself for
the baby's death. For one thing, her mother was pregnant at
the time, and about two months later Edna was introduced
to another baby brother, the one who later grew to be so
important to her.

It shouldn't be too hard to understand why Edna blamed
herself. She felt guilty not only because she caught whooping
cough at a time when she was supposed to be taking care of
her brother, but also because she couldn't forget that she had
wished him dead. Children who have such wishes—usually in
the sudden heat of fury, and, of course, they don't mean it—
are invariably horrified at their own power to cause such
dreadful things to happen when they do happen. She had
done wrong; she knew she had; and she felt that she was
alone responsible for what had happened. The result was that
she became overanxious to help with the new baby, because
she wanted to wipe out all the unpleasant memories of her
"crimes" against the first baby.

So she adored the new baby brother and never let him out
of her sight. Her parents weren't suspicious of her excessive
devotion to the baby because they thought it was "good for
her" and would take her mind off her "loss" of the other
child. (There is, of course, also the possibility that her parents were grateful to be relieved of some of the responsibilities that appeared with the new baby.)

"He learned how to read when he was three and a half,"
Edna said. "You can't tell me that that isn't real genius.
What's more, by the time he was five he was able to do as
much arithmetic as I knew at the age of ten. It was only that
the school system didn't believe in geniuses, or else he would

have graduated from high school when he was fourteen with all sorts of scholarships; he could have had his M.A. when he was twenty. He really has a *very* brilliant mind, and I have always respected and admired him for it."

"Who taught him to read?" her doctor asked her.

"Why, I did," she said. "I started drawing pictures of things for him to identify when he was about a year and a half old; things like 'house' and 'mouse' and 'bow-wow.' Then I drew the letters of the alphabet and he'd name them. I used to spend five or six hours a day with him, teaching him things, and he knew the entire alphabet by the time he was two and a half years old. He recited whole poems and he could do addition and subtraction."

It was her excessive devotion to him that made him precocious; there is no doubt about that. I knew a lawyer once who told me that he was somewhat frightened of his son. He and his wife had tried for fourteen years of their marriage to have a baby, until finally, when his wife was thirty-six and he thirty-eight, she became pregnant and they had a baby boy. His wife was a highly intelligent woman and a very gifted artist. She began to teach the child so assiduously, so very persistently, that he was able to read by the time he was two, and by the time he was three he was painting with oils. More than that, his I.Q. startled not only his parents but the psychologist who gave him the test when he was three and a half years old. "He's the first child I gave this test to," the psychologist told his parents, "who ever asked *me* questions."

My lawyer friend was frightened because he knew that his son displayed such aptitude only because of his mother's excessive preoccupation with him. The child was exposed to adult words, adult thinking, and adult mental exercising, including reading and all the rest of it, during almost every one of his waking hours, and, although my friend was proud of his son, he suspected that there might be some trouble ahead. If you remember, I discussed previously one of the difficulties in making children precocious: in effect, his wife was pushing their son through infancy and childhood too quickly. It's possible that their child has never had enough of childhood and that this may give him some trouble later on in life. My friend is not only worried about this prospect, but also about his wife's attachment to her son: it is an excessive devotion, far beyond what is good for the boy.

Edna had done exactly the same thing with her younger brother and in addition she had tried to make him as much like herself as possible, as if to re-create part of herself in him. She was trying to make herself over again, to be born again, to have another chance; this time she wouldn't make any mistakes, but would be The Good Child; she was convinced that in her present life she was The Bad Child. Now, this is fairly common. The reason that children frequently have dreams of having a twin is that they would like to be born over again, not only to be a good child, but to be a loved child, perhaps, or in an effort to correct their own mistakes and thus get approval.

It was only natural that Edna began to depend on her brother and love him to the extent that she did. There is another interesting thing that took place: at her brother's wedding she met the former husband of her new sister-in-law, and for the first time in her life she felt that she might be in love with a man. (She was then thirty-one.) He had everything for her, including great sexual attraction, which in itself was remarkable, inasmuch as she had never had any sexual feeling toward a man before.

This aspect of the case was easier to understand if one remembered that she felt such a strong attraction to her brother. There was this devious, unconscious pattern: she had repressed whatever sexual feelings she had toward her father and transferred them to her brother; of course, she had to repress her sexual feelings about him, too. By falling in love with her sister-in-law's ex-husband she was getting even with her for stealing her brother. Also, and what was more important, there was this development: how much of her sexual feeling for the man her sister-in-law had once been married to was really sexual feeling for the man her sister-in-law was married to now? This was the indirect way in which she could try to satisfy her sexual feelings for her brother, and she will be among the first to point out how very vicariously she gratified her sexual desires.

She would never have needed to become so attached to her brother if it hadn't been for her jealousy of the child who died. She was jealous of him, hated him, and wished that he were dead. When he died she was shocked at her own viciousness. She thought that she had caused his death, not only because she wished it on him, but also because she neglected him, so that he caught whooping cough and died. She outdid herself in her devotion to the next brother because she had to be forgiven for what she had done to the baby.

Edna's case had a happy ending. She became more mature, more aware of her real worth; eventually she married a man she met on a trip to South America (her first vacation alone). She didn't ask her brother if she should marry this man, because she was capable of making her own decisions; also, she now makes decisions for her children, too.

It might be worth while to discuss what her parents should have done to avoid her getting into such a mixed-up state of mind. First of all, she was given too much to do for her own good and for the good of the first baby. At the age of four she had a right to be jealous of him, and her parents made no attempt to talk it out with her. Even if she had loved the baby, taking care of him when she wanted to play would have aroused resentment. She didn't love him, and her resentment increased. As I said earlier, the older child should *want* to help and not do it just to get approval. Her parents didn't recognize that this was the motive behind her "love" for the second baby; enough approval would mean her "crime" was forgiven.

Also, her parents should have been suspicious of her great interest in her baby brother. She spent all of her time with him and built up a rather distorted social life for herself. To compensate for the lack of companions of her own age she had to treat her younger brother as a contemporary and give him credit for intelligence and wisdom beyond his years.

That's why she went to him for advice; she really fooled herself into believing that he was capable of advising her.

It's hard to say what her parents could have done to avoid the situation that came about. In the first place, Edna's mother was sick and had to have help with the baby. It's easy enough to suggest that the family get a governess for the baby, but how about a family that can't afford one?

The following answer is only a partial solution to the problem in some cases, but it works so wonderfully in most that I feel it should be given a try:

Children do lack an understanding of the economic problems and the practical difficulties that face their families. They can't see that just because a sled costs money they won't be able to have one. But they come through in a pinch, if an effort is made to give them simple, clear explanations of the situation. Parents should get these ideas across to the child: one—they are sympathetic; two—they know what she has been going through; three—they appreciate it (they should give her some rewards to show her they appreciate it); and four— things will work out to be better. This last is always true. If the child is impressed with the first three ideas, things *have* to be better. Above all, when parents are sympathetic it means that she will be encouraged to talk about her jealousy of the little one. She must know that her parents understand and that she has a right to be jealous. And neither parent should ever lecture the child about her "poor, tired mother," or her "overworked father," as a reason for taking care of the baby. It's unfair to make the family problems a dead weight on the child's enjoyment of life; one is running the risk of provoking more jealousy and having the child take out her resentment on the baby.

So many parents are at a loss when they are told to "love" their children more. It is a vague idea unless you realize that loving doesn't mean just a sentimental effusiveness: it's a real demonstration of consideration, fairness, sympathy, reassurance, kindness, and respect for a growing human being who has the feelings and emotions which are the basis of all human relations.

CHAPTER XII

Many Years Apart

—◆—

A CHILD who is born into a family where the other children are ten years old or more can be the most neglected of children or the best cared for. It depends on the older children to some extent, but again mostly on the parents. Too often when there is such a long interval between children the baby is unwanted; the parents refer to "an accident." Unwanted children have a way of finding it out, either from their parents' attitude or from the attitude of the other children, who have caught it from the parents. On the other hand, many parents want another baby when their older children have grown from young childhood. They may be more relaxed, in a better position financially to have a child, or it could be that they just love each other and babies enough to want another one. In such families the older children have been wanted, too, and loved, and one can be sure that jealousy is not much of a problem.

I have suggested that the arrival of the new baby should not be allowed to upset the established routine of the other children. Nine- and ten-year-olds have their own friends and their own interests and unless the baby is forced on them it won't be much of a threat to their security. The baby can be a source of amusement and fun to play with—but it won't be if it interferes too much with their other activities.

The problem of jealousy in children born years apart is less with the older ones than with the baby. Older children can understand their feelings better and usually know when they are loved by their parents; the effect the baby has on them ranges from mild to extreme annoyance. But the baby can suffer from their attitude toward it, which turns out to be our old enemy neglect. This was true in the case of Chris Griswold, who was born thirteen years after his sister and fifteen years after his older brother. (His story has been reconstructed from the things he told his psychiatrist.) The older children didn't look upon his arrival as a cause for jealousy; they were disgusted with him because they felt he had made their mother into something very unbecoming, even embarrassing. It didn't seem to them that it was proper that a woman of her age, with children their age, should have another child. It made them self-conscious, and it had in it elements of jealousy of both father and mother. Children can be jealous of their parents' sexual attractiveness for each other.

Children will be disturbed when they find evidence, or are inadvertent eyewitnesses, of sexual intercourse between their parents. When the Oedipus conflict is very strong—when the children are very young—this is understandable. But their disturbance is magnified when they are older and again find out that there has been sexual intercourse in their family; too many times their confusion is the fault of the parents. The children are not only jealous but are also embarrassed. The reason? Their parents may have neglected their sex education, or may have hinted that sex is dirty; in any case, the children get to think of sex as being dirty. What are they to believe, then, when they find out that their parents have been doing this dirty thing?

This was only one of the reasons Chris was resented by his brother and sister, so that he was a neglected child. After he was born his mother and father were bored with the whole idea and assigned the older children to take care of him, which they promptly refused to do. He grew up alone; he was an inadequate child because he never got enough care and never got enough help; he was backward in all of his schoolwork. The older brother and sister were very brilliant children, but he never had a chance to develop any of his talents. They were impatient with him and called him stupid. Gradually he began to believe that he *was* stupid.

His father was a high-school teacher who had retired after writing and publishing high-school textbooks. His textbooks were good, but it is doubtful if they would have become such a financial success if it had not been for Mrs. Griswold, who, through some connections at the state capitals and in Washington, managed to get Mr. Griswold's books accepted as official textbooks for the high schools of at least six states. From the time Mr. Griswold was thirty he was assured of a very excellent income for the rest of his life, inasmuch as each textbook had to be revised every year or so. New editions appeared frequently and more copies were sold. Chris's mother was an extremely aggressive and pushing sort of woman, while his father was very content to sit around and putter with his writing.

When Chris entered grammar school at the age of six his sister Emily was nineteen and going to college in their home town. His brother Felix, who was twenty-one, was at an out-of-town college doing post-graduate work. Chris tried to get Emily to help him, just as he had earlier tried to get her to play with him, when he was so lonely. And he was just as unsuccessful as he had always been. Chris was brought up by a succession of governesses, who came, stayed for a short while, found they couldn't stand the household, and left. What bothered them was the reversal of form: Mrs. Griswold was the boss, but she was often away on business trips. Mr. Griswold didn't know how to run the house, so nurses and maids and cooks came in rapid succession, leaving when the confusion got too great even for them.

Chris remembered that Emily had often told him how stupid he was because he couldn't learn the alphabet very quickly, and because he was unable to read by the time he got into the second grade. At the same time his father would constantly remind him that Emily and Felix were able to read before they even entered kindergarten. He finally discovered that it was useless to try to get help from anyone at home. He was left back in the second grade just long enough for Mrs. Griswold to find out about it. She marched down to the school herself and, by turning on the same persuasiveness that convinced those six states to adopt her husband's textbooks for their high schools, proved to the principal that Chris was not only old enough for the third grade, but should actually be put in the fourth grade! Well, he was put in the fourth grade and was even more completely lost there than he was in the second grade, where he learned only a few things, and quite slowly.

Because the fourth grade was way beyond him, so were the activities of his classmates. Besides, they despised him a little because they knew how he got promoted and skipped. His new teacher soon found that he was completely inadequate to the work. When she called on Chris's mother to tell her, she was browbeaten into tutoring Chris an hour a day, without pay. So Chris was exposed to the shame of having to be tutored and worked-over specially by his teacher, which made him even more despicable in the eyes of his classmates, because now he was really "Teacher's Pet." This was a college town and the fathers of many of the children were professors. They were intelligent children, who were also given a lot of help. The competition would have been keen for any child; it was absolutely overwhelming for Chris, with all the drawbacks that he had to face. A child who is exposed to proof of his inadequacy day after day, class after class, will be convinced that he is inadequate the rest of his life.

Chris was in a still rockier boat. He had a whole family of models of intelligence to live up to, whose pride wouldn't let them admit that Chris was as inadequate as he thought he was. He was pushed still harder and graduated from high school without knowing the seven times table.

His feelings about himself were also influenced by his sexual life. When he was five his mother caught him masturbating and gave him a long lecture on the wickedness of what he had been doing. He was thoroughly frightened and convinced that there must be something wrong with him to make him do such an evil thing. However, the sensation was pleasant and he was lonely enough so that he resorted to it again and again, each time feeling more and more guilty. One day his sister Emily caught him masturbating; she was shocked and horrified even more than his mother and told him it was the reason for his difficulties: masturbation, she said, affected the brain. This effect on *his* brain was what made him so stupid. Of course, it isn't so—but Chris thought it was and he remembered it for the rest of his life. As he grew older he added sexual fantasies to his daydreams and continued to masturbate, so that each time he had an orgasm the pleasantness of the sensation would be followed by a feeling of disgust and self-condemnation. He felt degraded and he had great contempt for himself.

His daydreams and fantasies seemed to compensate him for his failures in living. He needed this support; he created it from within himself because he had decided he couldn't get it from anyone else. Finding the fantasy world much more pleasant and comfortable, he withdrew completely from the world of reality. His feelings of unworthiness and self-blame were so strong and so burdensome that he couldn't face living with real people.

Chris was one of those people who refuse to fight back and won't use even a small amount of normal aggressiveness to hold their own. These are timid and shy people; they are called asocial by their friends. Psychiatric books have many other names for it. They live in a vicious circle in which they feel useless and inferior because they don't do anything worth while and they can't do anything worth while because they feel useless and inferior. Chris didn't go to college; instead, he got a job as a service-station attendant, which was further proof to himself and to his brilliant family that he was just an inadequate person. The Griswolds were very happy when he was about to be drafted, because they thought it would "make a man of him," and they were chagrined and ashamed when he was declared 4-F because of psychoneurotic difficulties. The psychiatrist at the induction center was able to find out in thirty minutes what his family couldn't learn in twenty years: Chris needed help.

It was during his visits to the psychoanalyst that Chris became aware of his lifelong feelings of insecurity and his low self-esteem. He began to see how dependent he had been and how he had been unable to face reality. It had started with the feeling that he was an unwanted child and he grew up to feel that it was his inadequacy which made him unwanted. The neglected child looks upon neglect as punishment for something he has done that is bad, or punishment for not being good enough.

In the story of Chris and his family we can see some of the things which can make life unhappy for the child born years after the next older brother or sister. For one thing, the older children were adolescents when the baby was born. Their normal interest in sex and in their parents' sex relations especially was distorted by the fact that they had been told that sex was wicked and bad. Adolescents normally cannot understand what their parents see in each other; if they feel that sex is shameful it may make them feel that babies are shameful and undesirable.

Children's interests change and develop as they grow older. Adolescents don't usually want to take care of a baby; they may do baby sitting for a neighbor, but you shouldn't expect them to enjoy cleaning up after a sibling who interferes with their lives. Chris's parents didn't want to take care of the baby, yet they demanded that the older children do a job that they themselves considered tiresome!

David Clinton, who was eleven when his baby brother arrived, would never hold the infant, or even touch him. He was particularly squeamish about going near the baby's room when diapers had to be changed. (Many grown men who don't have babies of their own feel this way, too.) Later on, when the younger boy was about five, David enjoyed him tremendously, took him to baseball games, helped him construct wooden toys in the playroom, and even took him along occasionally on trips with his own friends.

If David's mother had insisted on his helping with the baby, or showing some obvious form of "love" for his brother, she might have provoked a lot of jealousy. Instead, she took care of the baby herself and never allowed him to become a nuisance to the older boy. Many times that first year she said to David: "Yes, David, I know you feel a little disgusted with the baby, and you feel envious, too. Don't worry about it. I still think you're a wonderful boy. You needn't take care of the baby or hold him; that's what mothers are for; it's my job, and I love him just as I love you." David slowly began to show a sneaking interest in the baby; when he came home after school he'd ask his mother rather casually how the baby was. She even caught him making funny faces at the baby to make him laugh; he didn't know he was being watched. Gradually David forgot that he was ever jealous, or that there was a time when his brother didn't exist.

Frances, a self-conscious girl of sixteen, counts on Harold, her seven-year-old brother, to break the ice when her friends gather at her home. Her boy friends go right into the nursery when they arrive and start tinkering with the electric train, and it helps them get off to a gay evening. When Harold gets too noisy and excited, his parents very gently take him off to bed. Sometimes Frances calls him a pest—usually when she is busy and doesn't want to be interrupted. But he knows that she really likes him, and Frances does like him, because she doesn't feel that he is a burden or that she has to have him with her constantly.

Frances was nine when her brother was born. She helped buy things for his layette and was very much interested in her mother's pregnancy. However, a month after the baby came home she became morose, depressed, and sullen. She fought off the kind advances her mother made toward her, and she was coy and clinging when her father was around. Her parents knew that something was wrong and, because she was closer to her father than to her mother, it was decided that he should talk to her about her jealousy. He did. Then he took her out and bought her a new dress, took her to a musical comedy that she wanted to see, and convinced her that she was a thoroughly delightful companion. They both bought trinkets for the baby. When Frances took hers into the living room where her mother and the baby were sitting, she suddenly threw her arms about her mother and kissed her—the first spontaneous gesture of affection in several weeks.

Her father and mother agreed that Frances should be given special consideration for a while and should not have to take any responsibility for the baby. Her mother also talked to Frances about her jealousy and assured her that every child with a baby brother felt the same way about him. Her mother also pointed out that children do not fully understand grown-up love-making and that fathers loved their children in a different way, but in a very real way. Frances admitted that she had felt funny when she thought that her father had had intercourse with her mother. As the year progressed, she became devoted to a certain movie idol; she told her father not to kiss her when her friends were around. She indicated very strongly that he had better confine his demonstrations of love to her mother! Soon after this she began to be interested in Harold: she was able to accept him as another member of the household.

It's important to remember that the jealous child knows that he is jealous. It doesn't make much difference if the children are only a year apart, or if they are ten years apart: there will be jealousy anyway. The seriousness of the problem depends on its coming out into the open, so that the child will not feel guilty and will not feel that he is abnormal because he is jealous. It is not at all to the child's everlasting discredit that he knows whenever someone is taking something away from him, especially something he needs, like the love and understanding of his parents. Once he is convinced that he is not wicked and that his parents still love him, any child, at no matter what age, will be better able to develop friendliness rather than hatefulness toward his brothers and sisters.

CHAPTER XIII

Rivalry between the Sexes

———◆———

WHEN a girl is jealous of her brother it isn't just because of the biological differences between them. She is jealous because she thinks her parents love her brother more than they love her.

No one is denying that the physical differences between boys and girls—later, men and women—are decidedly in favor of men. Women menstruate, bear children, and then go through menopause, or change of life; these are three characteristics of women which can put them at a disadvantage in competition with men. These functions are time-consuming, painful, and to many women annoying. However, to say that being physically handicapped at times *must* make women feel inferior is like saying that any physical defect, even in a man, has to make *him* feel inferior.

We know that there are many physically handicapped people who don't go through life envious of every healthy person: with proper training and understanding these people can learn to live with their troubles and not feel that they have to resent everyone who is in good health. That there aren't more well-adjusted people among the great number of physically handicapped is due to the lack of proper training and handling of the problem. In the same way, the girl who is depressed, bitter, and resentful because, being a woman, she has to suffer while her brother, being a man, doesn't, can be helped out, too: she doesn't have to grow up feeling inferior and jealous.

It isn't easy. Our culture is based on a changing concept

of the role of women, and our daughters are caught up in the middle of it. A woman these days doesn't have to be as whole-hearted or drudgelike a housewife as women were fifty years ago; in the home she can turn on switches, push buttons, and take advantage of all the inventions that make house-work—and even motherhood—less difficult than it was then. When she marries she isn't expected to have more than two or three children, and she finds she has time for something else besides the career of being a wife and a mother.

What else can she do? What other career has she been trained for? And what can we do about her feelings of in-feriority to men? It is the idea that they are inferior which makes women feel hopeless about competing with men; par-ents are still bringing up their daughters to be good wives and mothers and to be subservient to their husbands. Not that there's anything wrong with being a good wife and mother. It's just that the wife and mother today and perhaps in the future doesn't have to weave cloth, make clothes, can food, and work on the farm with her husband while she is trying to bring up her children. She has more time to herself; occa-sionally she has as much time as her husband.

If a woman prefers to make her job in the family her career, she can become adjusted to it. Some women prefer large families with lots of work: it makes them feel they are fulfilling their function as women. And some women can't become successful in careers outside of the home because there is a sort of stigma attached to *not* fulfilling one's func-tion as a woman. "There must be something wrong," some-one says, "if a woman denies herself marriage and having children." And yet, as we know and can see all around us, women are being educated to compete with men. Some of them become successful, happy—and remain non-neurotic. These are the women who don't feel at a disadvantage be-cause men have sexual appendages that are supposed to make them superior beings; they are women who don't look on their female biological functions as a hindrance to all activ-ity outside of child-bearing.

In the same way that the less intelligent, less handsome, less strong child can feel less loved—and jealous—the girl in a family can feel less loved than her brothers. Again, it depends on the parents and their attitudes toward their children: mothers seem to favor their sons and fathers their daughters. Sometimes the parents reverse themselves, but it's a natural process and there is little parents can do to avoid jealousy of either the girls or the boys (for the boys may feel their sisters are getting the advantages) unless they are extremely careful to avoid showing favoritism toward any one group.

Because of the differences between the sexes, jealousy is exaggerated during adolescence. That is when girls become aware for the first time that there are functions of womanhood which set them apart from their brothers. Boys become interested in other girls and demand more freedom. At such a time the daughters can become aware, for the first time, that there are things the sons are permitted to do which they cannot do. They resent the differences in the hours they and their brothers are allowed to keep and they are very apt to blame it on the fact that their physical differences make them inferior and less loved. Or, the boys may be jealous of the greater number of clothes their sisters get, which they may interpret as more love. And, finally, there may even be definite proof that one parent or the other is playing favorites. Any of these things may help convince boys that girls are better, or cause too much resentment in girls by making them feel boys are better.

I have mentioned the process of identification, or imitation. After all, how do boys grow up to be men and how do girls grow up to be women? They learn to be like their parents; they love and admire their parents, and they believe them to be models whom they should imitate. The parents are the people who give or hold back approval; a child who imitates a parent completely can naturally expect nothing but approval from that parent. In the normal family group, therefore, no matter how strong the tendency is for children to be attached to the parent of the opposite sex, the love, respect, and admiration for the parent of the same sex makes the child model himself or herself on that parent.

Parents must also consider the normal developmental pattern which takes place in every child. A little boy until he is five or six is close to his mother and imitates many of the things which she does. He helps her in the kitchen, puts on her lipstick occasionally, refuses to get a haircut. In nursery school he plays house along with the girls, sets the table, puts the babies to bed, and so on. That is completely normal, accepted behavior; no mother would consider it feminine, or tease the child for his actions.

Little girls like to wear overalls simply because they are more comfortable. They climb as well as boys, play at building houses, and pretend to be bombardiers in make-believe bombers; their toy shelves are usually stocked with the same blocks and cars which a boy has. Gradually they shift over to more feminine things: they want pretty shoes like their mothers', or they insist on carrying a pocketbook to school. They ask their fathers to admire their new dresses and they pretend they have breasts like their mothers'. (They may stuff things into their sweaters to produce the effect.) This growth and behavior change is normal and sound. Some girls develop physically more slowly than other girls and their identification may take a longer time to evolve, but almost overnight a tomboy can change to a feminine young lady. A girl may look almost indistinguishable from her male companions during the day and at night blossom out into a very exotic and seductive-looking young miss.

Jealousy, of course, may accentuate and prolong any one of these stages. It need not be at all upsetting, if there are two parents both of whom like their roles and continue to give the child admiration and attention. A girl may become a more accomplished baseball player because she wants more attention from her father, but with a wise father she will soon discover that she gets approval without having to work for it; not only that, she will drop her baseball playing very quickly if a male her own age whom she likes shows his disapproval.

When a little boy becomes aware of the difference between male and female roles, his shift takes place gradually away from his imitation of his mother and toward identification with his father. *It does not take place all at once,* nor does any phase of growing up. Over a summer he may exhibit fondness for his father's interest in swimming, or fishing, or chopping trees. Then he goes back to school and, because he is a little unsure of his standing in the group, may spend several afternoons following his mother around and clinging to her. She will not make him into a "Mama's boy" if she spends this time with him, or gives him added attention. Love is not just for girls, and attention from the mother is needed heavily by both sexes.

There is one more aspect of this normal growth pattern that parents should consider. A girl who is temperamentally like her father, who is interested, let us say, in scientific experiments, or who has a muscular ability which her mother does not possess, may identify in part with those things which her father enjoys. She may want to go off on long hikes because she likes it, she does it well, and her father enjoys it, too. This does not mean that she is rejecting her feminine role, nor does it mean that she will become a mannish sort of woman. A boy who cannot bear mathematics, but who is artistic or musical, like his mother, needn't necessarily be considered feminine when he identifies with her aesthetic interests. The danger lies in his father's or mother's disapproval of his interest, their convincing him that he isn't manly because he doesn't want to play on a football team.

It is obvious, therefore, that parents should let the child grow normally, and not force him, either by neglect or by shaming him, to adopt a sex role *at any stage* which is contrary to his sex or his level of maturity. Nor should they disapprove or reject a child's interests and skill which may not be according to the traditional ideas of what is masculine or feminine. Many of the old ideas about what men do and don't do and what women do and don't do are changing. Fathers are taking care of babies—changing diapers, feeding and bathing them—and helping in housekeeping without losing status as males. Indeed, it appears that this sharing of family activities may be the beginning of a more companionable and satisfying marriage than the old rigid division into women's duties and men's duties.

A fatherly father, who recognizes that his son's mission in life is to become a man, will be very smart to help him along and not permit his masculine pride in the adoration of his daughters to blind him against his son's need for attention and approval. The wise mother will encourage her son, as he grows up, to seek masculine companionship and to get help, preferably from his father. She will not hold on to him just because her daughters have all deserted her for their father; nor will she allow herself to be swayed by her need for companionship, or any idea that her son can supply that companionship to her.

Wherever there is jealousy because a girl thinks she is inferior to boys because of her physical and biological functions, it is necessary to emphasize that there are differences in the children and that they must become aware of the differences. One of the best ways of meeting penis envy is for mothers to show little girls that the feminine role is desirable. Mothers can do this best by enjoying motherhood and womanhood. Also, all the children—both boys and girls— should be given a clear statement of how we function sexually, emphasizing the importance of the differences between men and women.

No matter what the reason, even if there is extreme jealousy present, in most cases parents needn't worry too much if their children imitate the opposite sex in early childhood. Usually they outgrow the tomboyishness or girlish behavior by adolescence. They become interested in competing with other children outside the family—sometimes because they give up trying to compete at home—so they are more willing to accept the self-imposed limitations of their own sex. Boys will join other boys and girls will become interested in feminine things for the first time.

It is never desirable to make children feel that they are all the same, with the same potentialities in either their sex or their other physical capacities. We are all different, whether in our social lives or in our sexual roles. Make the children feel that you value their individuality, their skills, and their maleness or femaleness. Give them a chance to explore their abilities in various ways—in music, in science, in crafts. They won't want to do the same things. They'll be glad to find areas of achievement where they are good and where they can feel satisfied. Never act as if you, the parent, are omnipotent. You are not, and the child will discover it soon enough. Appreciate what they do that is different from what you can do, and remember, *no rewards* for being able to sew "as well as Mother," or to read "as well as your older brother." Every child, no matter how seemingly inept, has some capabilities. Help him to find them, and you will be helping to give him a sense of his own importance at the same time that you are minimizing, or removing, the causes of jealousy.

You will remember that I emphasized earlier the importance of being honest with your children—honest about your love for your spouse and your love for *all* your children. This is extremely important in the process of identification. When parents love each other, the child will grow to accept it; he will have a pattern of living and loving to guide him in his later adult life. Even when he shows jealousy of his father, gentle, loving reassurance will make him feel better. As he grows toward adolescence, he will have this pattern of affection and tenderness between men and women, boys and girls, to guide him. Information about sex is not enough. He must be inspired by the respect and love for each other that you show in family relationships.

CHAPTER XIV

Stepparents and Stepchildren

———◆———

THE CHILD in the "broken home"—whether the home is broken by death or by divorce—can find at least two more reasons to be jealous: the new parent, should his own father or mother remarry, and the stepbrothers or sisters the stepparent may bring into the family. The problems of jealousy can complicate the unhappiness that began when the home broke up. Some children never quite recover from it; at best it takes a very exceptional person to make up to a child for the loss of the other parent. Very few adults who have had to go through the experience of death or divorce are emotionally able to handle their own feelings, let alone those of the child. It would be wiser, in most cases, if the parent got professional help.

Children who live with a single parent may make what appears to be a satisfactory adjustment until the parent decides to remarry. Then, to everyone's amazement, the children may become so antagonistic to the plan that the wedding may never take place. There are many reasons why children feel this way, and we are concerned now with the way in which jealousy plays a part in it. For one thing, there is the children's unwillingness to have anyone disturb the relationship which has grown up between them and the single parent. Bringing home a new parent can be as great a blow as bringing home a new baby brother, unless the children are adequately prepared for it and handled wisely afterward.

We often hear of women—and men—who are so easily intimidated by their children that they never do remarry. One such woman, a widow, had defied her parents to marry the man of her choice, but didn't remarry because her children objected to all her beaux. The reason is obvious. She married in the first place in order to rid herself of her parents, so she wouldn't have to listen to *them*. But she was afraid she would lose her children by not giving in to their wishes, so she obeyed them. We can be suspicious of so much self-sacrifice, because, nine times out of ten, the children could use a new and fairly competent father, no matter how much they object. Such women like their sacrifices: it is as if they accumulate unhappiness for themselves in order to run up a big bill for their children to pay back. It becomes one of those debts children owe that they can never repay—although they may never stop trying. The mother never stops dunning them; she will remind them over and over again of the gray hairs they have given her, of her wrinkles, her unhappiness—and of the men she could have married, but no, her children needed her, she thought. If she had known then what she knows now . . . she will say; if she had only known her children would be so unappreciative, etc., etc.

It may be that those children who are left with only one parent find some part, at least, of their problems simplified. Consider this: where there are two parents the children compete with each other for the favors of both, as well as with one parent for the affection of the other. Then, too, there is the added complication of jealousy in the parents themselves, who may not be above trying to win over one child or the other. This sort of competition in parents is more serious where there has been a divorce and each parent, in his or her own home, vies with the other to get the exclusive affection and respect of the children.

Special problems come up depending on whether the remaining parent has been divorced or widowed. Let us look at what complications are to be considered when one parent has died. For example, one must always find out if the child feels guilty about the death of the parent, like the boy in

Chapter VII, who blamed himself for his father's death because he had wished so often that his father would die. This isn't at all unusual; much older people can feel this way, too. One could go into a long philosophical discourse about our cultural concepts of grief, and how it is a mixture of feelings of guilt (when we tend to search ourselves to find if we had anything to do with the death of the departed one) and extreme dependency (when we find ourselves deprived of a person on whom we can no longer be dependent).

It's difficult for the surviving parent to think about the effect the death of the other parent has on the children, because the parent who survives has his or her own problems to deal with; sometimes there just isn't enough time for a bereaved person to think of much beyond his or her own personal grief. However, it could help the parent to pay some attention to the children's grief. We all know how easily our own troubles slip off our shoulders when we become interested in the troubles of others.

Occupational therapy means treatment by the use of work. The work, of course, is intended to divert the mind from the immediate and more troublesome problem. The care that a mother gives her children when the father has died is a form of occupational therapy for the mother; the treatment is not only beneficial to her, but extremely important to the children.

The loss of a loved parent deprives the child of someone on whom he can be dependent. This shows itself very clearly in the child's extreme dependency on the remaining parent. Of course, things are much harder for that parent, because not only does she have to cope with her own grief, but she has to deal with all the responsibilities which were formerly divided between two parents. For a person who has never shown much real responsibility toward her children, their sudden increased dependency on her will cause her some trouble. Such a parent will immediately want to run out and find someone to share this burden and she will run into more difficulties; to her amazement, she will find that her children are entirely opposed to the entrance of anyone else into the family group.

There are some who think that children become more resentful and less tolerant of a parent's attempts to remarry when a long time elapses after the death of the other parent, during which the children have become quite possessive of the surviving parent. If this were all that mattered, if we didn't take into account the parent's personal wishes, the safest procedure would be for a parent to remarry—if she had any intentions of doing so—as soon as possible after the death of her spouse. It is not only that the children get used to having a surviving parent to themselves and subsequently feel more possessive about her, but also that they tend to think of the deceased parent in a more and more complimentary and flattering way as time goes on. The memory of a dead mother or father becomes suffused with very kindly, charitable, and generous feelings; this new picture of the deceased parent makes it harder for any stranger who would like to take his place.

There was a broken home situation in a private school which came to the attention of the school psychiatrist because of the behavior of the children. In this case the father, a widower, didn't remarry. The two children were Larry, who was seven, and Lynn, who was five, and there never were two more rebellious and undisciplined children. Larry masturbated openly and defiantly; he disrupted his classroom sessions by his constant attempts to put on a show; he threw his food around in the lunchroom; and he fought with the other children, who disliked him intensely. Lynn was a sweet-looking child, but she was almost as poisonous as her brother. It was decided that both children should be dropped from the school if the home situation couldn't be cleared up.

The trouble was that the father was a very ineffectual, although well-meaning, man. He was so very thoughtful of his children that he would fire nurses and maids—even those who might have stayed on at risk of life and limb—at the slightest provocation—usually simply because Larry or Lynn

objected. The result was that there was a succession of girls
and women who paraded in and out of the children's lives.
They would come in smiling hopefully and go away angry.
The children never had any discipline because they were
able to do anything they wanted. They actually did the
hiring and firing. When a new maid or governess arrived she
would be subjected to a three-way interview, and the impression she made on the children counted more than the father's
opinion of her experience and ability.

In addition, Larry was jealous of Lynn's so-called sweetness. Most maids and nurses were more interested in her and
showed it, which infuriated Larry. He was very open about it.
"You're always taking her side," he would say, and throw
something at the nurse. On the other hand, if the poor maid
or nurse would try to show Larry some consideration Lynn
would have a tantrum. Nevertheless, despite their jealousy of
each other, the two would unite against the common enemy.

These children were uncontrolled and uncontrollable.
Their lack of respect for any authority carried over into
school and the father was warned, at a conference with the
teachers, that he would have to do something about putting
his foot down, or else. He was told about the children's need
for a firm hand and he was advised to disregard their wishes
in the matter of choosing a nurse. He was also warned that
he must not, under any circumstances, fire a nurse just because one child or the other complained about her. This
isn't advice one gives to *every* parent: the complaints of most
children should be taken seriously most of the time. However, Lynn and Larry were too spoiled and too prejudiced to
be able to give an unbiassed opinion of any nurse's ability.
The nurse who was finally picked has been there for a year,
and there has been definite improvement. They were not
too popular with the other children even after their improvement was noticeable to the teachers, but after some
prodding and explaining to the others they were permitted
to join them.

Why had they acted the way they did? Mostly because they

had suffered a great loss when their mother died. No one had tried to explain to them why they were unhappy. They took it for granted that this was a hostile world from which they could only expect to be hurt, so they defied it. They should have been helped to express their feelings and they should have been reassured that their father would try to care for them and protect them. Instead, not understanding, they blamed their father for their mother's death, punishing him for their loss; they protected themselves psychologically with an attitude of resentment and defiance, and they were suspicious of each other.

Their father became over-permissive in an attempt to help them, but it only increased their bewilderment and antagonism. It was as if they were saying: "You can't bribe us; we are loyal to our mother whom you took away from us." When they fought against discipline, they needed it most. Children are much happier with someone who can control them, especially when they learn that the rules and regulations they have to live under protect them, too.

It is common knowledge to psychiatrists, judges in juvenile courts, wise teachers, and understanding parents that children who show antisocial behavior are, in most instances, covering up the hurts and bruises they have received. The treatment for such disturbed children is usually wise and firm guidance, as well as trying to find out what bothers them. That's why talking to children about their grief is desirable. Making them feel understood will leave them less liable to deep jealousy and antagonism if the surviving parent should marry again, or even if he should introduce a new housekeeper or nurse. Children who are disturbed by the loss of a parent will be more suspicious and watchful of each other, more jealous of any extra attention that either receives. Any favoritism will be taken as one more example of the world's unfairness. There is no better way to guard against bitterness and jealousy than by talking things over with them and bringing everything out into the open.

This is one of those rare situations in dealing with children when it is better to take their attitudes with a grain of salt. Their jealousy of their exclusive rights will, of course, make them want very much to keep their parent to themselves; they will prefer that he remain single and devote his time to their own family unit. It doesn't seem to matter to them that the loneliness of a widowed parent should be considered, that very loneliness which makes the parent more dependent upon them. It might come as a blow to children to learn that their father, for example, doesn't find enough happiness in his children—because that's what is implied when a parent feels he wants to remarry—and has to go to a stranger for the happiness he thinks is his right. The only time that the children have to be considered is in relation to the effect of the new parent on them, in the ability of the new parent to understand and love the children despite the difficulties that stand in his way. He needs more than ordinary kindliness: it's a situation which calls for a master tactician, one with a great understanding of the problems that the children are faced with and, above all, a sense of humor.

Children need two parents, whether they know it or not, and in the long run it would be far better to overlook their objections and supply them with someone who is capable of substituting for the missing parent, and knows what he has to do. This is especially difficult when the children are in their teens. The mother or father is not yet forty and many years have elapsed since the death or divorce of the spouse. After meeting a sympathetic and understanding person, the parent begins to think of getting married again. There is opposition from the children, sometimes subtle and hard to recognize—or it may be expressed in cruel remarks about the aging lovers, or it may even be open rebellion. Such a reaction is usually based on jealousy: the children envy their parent's romance.

The result of the marriage can be of great benefit to the children, depending on the new parent. Girls of teen age especially need the companionship and counseling of an understanding and sympathetic mother, even if she is not their real mother. But such a marriage can only be successful if the woman entering into this closely knit and single-minded family group is fully aware of the job ahead of her. She has to break down long-lived, deep-seated prejudices against her, she has to cope with the exaggerated picture the children have of their dead mother, and she has to overcome their resentment of anyone who seems to be robbing them of some part, at least, of their father's love.

As if this weren't enough, there can also be the added problem which arises when the new parent has children of her own; the complications which follow appear to be completely insurmountable. Added to their resentment of a father who has proven to be faithless to them, there arrives a new threat to their security in the form of some hateful children who may be of their own age (the offspring of the intruder who has made off with their father) and obviously they are going to be forced to love these upstarts, or else incur their father's wrath and disapproval. You can easily see how much more difficult this problem can be than one in which there is jealousy between children of the same mother and father; the situation becomes even more difficult because of the natural protectiveness of the new parent. She will feel more inclined to favor her own children, so that, unless everyone is extremely careful, the new marriage can end up a good deal less than happily.

The addition of stepbrothers and stepsisters to a family brings together individuals who may distrust each other. They will watch very carefully to see that the other side is not going to gain any advantage over them. Many times these children are exactly the same age and the clashes that take place between them are much more severe than if the children were widely separated in age. The children jealously guard their own advantages and run for protection to the head of the group: the wife's children run to her, and the husband's children, of course, to him. It would be a heartless parent who couldn't find even a little justice in the protests of his or her own children. So, as the children oppose each other, they can't help but embroil their parents in the argument; what starts out as jealousy between children becomes more complicated by the entrance of the parents, each one of whom is forced to take sides. Eventually the marriage may break down.

Or, take the case of a widowed or divorced mother who marries a man with superior children, so that there is a great contrast between her husband's children and her own. If she isn't wise she may make her own children compete with her husband's children, holding the latter up as examples in order to make her own children study more, even though they don't have as high I.Q.'s as the others. The result is jealousy in some form or other. Where there is jealousy between stepbrothers and stepsisters, it can usually be traced to the parents' playing favorites.

The woman who brings her children to a husband who has children of his own should be prepared to love his children as much as hers. It's exactly as if she were adopting his children; incidentally, they have to adopt her, too.

Judy was in such a position. Her father, a widower, remarried when she was only a year and a half old. As she grew up she got all the love her stepmother could give her; as far as Judy was concerned this was her real mother, for she was the only mother Judy ever knew. Judy was seven when the new baby was born.

In school Judy began to steal things. She stole from lockers, coat pockets, and from the other children's handbags. It got so that whenever anything was missing all one had to do was to look in Judy's pocketbook or in her locker. Her stepmother was called for a conference and it was decided that Judy probably needed more attention. Because this had worked before with other children, the school psychiatrist suggested that it might not be a bad idea if the mother brought Judy to school herself, rather than send her by bus. She did, and the stealing soon stopped. Judy got more attention at home and was so well adjusted that she could be told, when she was eight, that this wasn't her real mother. The problem was exactly the same as when adopted children have to be told of their origin; Judy could take it.

When Judy was twelve and her half brother was five, her mother overheard this conversation:

"I know something, Judy," he said to her. "I came from Mummy's tummy, but you didn't. You came from somebody else's tummy."

"I know that," said Judy. "But Mummy loved me longer than she loved you."

Judy's stepmother needs no more proof that she has done a good job of showing Judy that she is loved, nor does she ever have to worry about letting the truth come out accidentally that Judy is not her real daughter.

There is little doubt in the minds of some students in the field of family relations that the bad effects on the children are the most important consideration in the question of divorce. It is hard for a child to make up his mind whether or not to favor father or mother. Sometimes he is forced to make a quick decision. It's very obvious that he won't like whatever decision he makes, because he will be disapproved of by either his father or his mother, so that he may end up with a good deal of anxiety.

In looking into the situation where divorced parents play favorites and try to outdo each other to get the love of the children, one has to consider jealousy between the parents as well as jealousy between the children. The children may divide into groups. There are no hard and fast rules, and there are many reasons for some children to favor the mother, others, the father. Mostly there is the familiar pattern of the boys lining up on the mother's side and the girls on the father's side, but sometimes, surprisingly enough, the girls may feel that the mother has been put upon. For example, if the father has been unfaithful to the mother, the women may align themselves against their common enemy, man, although the daughters may have loved their father very much. The children's problems are increased when the divorced parents openly or insidiously try to take advantage of their "divided custody" of the children.

One rather sad little boy, Philip, who is now seven, was the innocent victim of such a campaign by his father, who was trying to work out his own feelings of revenge through his child. There was a rather messy divorce and Philip spent most of the year with his father, and only two two-week sessions and every other Saturday with his mother, who had remarried. The boy's father was permitted to send along Fräulein or Mademoiselle, whichever was taking care of the boy, so that he got complete reports on the goings-on at his ex-wife's home. He exaggerated these reports and sent her long telegrams—they lived in the same city—complaining bitterly of her behavior. Once, on a rainy Saturday, she took the boy to a children's theater play and that night she got the following wire:

AM INFORMED THAT PHILIP WENT OUTDOORS WITHOUT OVERSHOES AND WAS DRIVEN IN YOUR CONVERTIBLE WHICH HAS TWO LEAKY PLACES IN THE ROOF. ALSO, HE WAS TAKEN TO DRAUGHTY AUDITORIUM WHERE AT LEAST SIX CHILDREN WERE COUGHING. PLEASE INFORM ME IF YOU HAVE ANY INTENTION OF TAKING PROPER CARE OF MY SON.

Philip was really very fond of his mother, despite his father's propaganda against her. However, he was only barely tolerant of his stepfather, and usually was very insulting to him. Luckily the stepfather was an indulgent man who understood the boy's resentment and didn't try to complicate the problem by forcing himself on the boy.

"I feel he has to work this out for himself," the stepfather said, "and nothing I can do or say will help him. But I do wish he'd stop staring at me, every time he comes over, as if I were about to snort fire and smoke."

When Philip was about five his mother and stepfather became the parents of a baby boy. They had their first inkling of Philip's feelings when he came to visit them a week after his mother came home from the hospital with the baby. He became suddenly very destructive and tore up a number of his stepfather's valuable stamp albums. He made open gestures of defiance when his stepfather mildly reproved him, then kicked and bit him and his mother; he finished up by pushing a floor lamp over on the baby's crib. Mademoiselle couldn't stand it any longer then and confessed that Philip had been the victim of a campaign by his father. He had been told over and over again that his mother didn't really love him. To prove it, his father pointed out that she was having the baby for only one reason: Philip wasn't important enough to her. The boy was taught to be jealous of his baby half brother and showed his jealousy by his destructiveness. When this story and the telegrams were shown in court, the judge this time awarded major custody of Philip to his mother and stepfather. Philip has begun to like his half brother now that his father isn't around to poison his mind.

Not all parents are so vicious; divorces take place where husband and wife don't try to get even with each other. When the Parsons' divorced they thought enough of their children's welfare to want to help them ease their problems. What happened was this: Mr. Parsons was given custody of the children, because his wife married a man with a child of his own. Mr. Parsons realized that his children needed their real mother as much as they needed their real father. There were, for a short time, signs that they were becoming jealous of their new stepbrother. By a stroke of luck the two households were only a block away from each other, so that the children were permitted to spend each afternoon with their mother and stepfather. Both parents felt the children needed to get the reassurance that would come from knowing that their mother still loved them, even if they were not with her all the time. Their jealousy of the stepbrother wore down to nothing.

Children who are brought together by remarraige of their respective parents should be encouraged to be friends. They should never be ordered to love each other—or the new parent. The children should not be told they are really brothers and sisters, or that they shouldn't show antagonism or jealousy. They will—and they'll feel freer and easier about it, less guilty (perhaps less than real brothers and sisters, in fact), if they are not under pressure to "love" one another. And one should never try to persuade the children to accept the stepparent as a substitute for the missing one. The new parent is not the same thing; he is a friend who is interested in the children's well-being and he must convince them of that with a friendly, patient attitude.

Children will have a greater problem with jealousy because of the loss of a parent. It takes several years if the children are older, though not too long if the children are small, to help them adjust to the situation, but friendliness and kindness are still the most effective way of preventing long-lasting jealousy.

CHAPTER XV

Twins and the Importance
of Avoiding Comparisons

———◆———

DR. SAMUEL JOHNSON felt very strongly on the subject of comparing children to each other. He believed that whipping was preferable: "I would rather have the rod to be the general terror of all . . ." he once said, "than tell a child, if you do thus and thus you will be more esteemed than your brothers and sisters. . . . By exciting emulation and comparisons of superiority, you lay the foundation of lasting mischief; you make brothers and sisters hate each other."

Parents are unaware of the dangerous possibilities of the habit, usually the result of an attempt to get one child to equal the output of the other, or be as quiet as, or as bright as, or as well trained to the toilet as the other. They would like to teach the one child by getting him to imitate the other, and mere imitation has always been the hardest and most ineffectual way to learn anything, even though it looks easy.

"Why can't you be helpful like Ferdie?" a mother may say to the younger brother, Martin. Or, "Why can't you be as obedient [or as clean, or as studious] as Ferdie?" It's obvious to Martin that his mother loves Ferdie more because Ferdie *is* better in all these things and that if Martin wants his mother to love him he has to equal or exceed Ferdie. But Martin *knows* that Ferdie isn't always helpful or good and that many times his mother has been taken in by Ferdie. For instance, when both have been playing noisily Ferdie is the one who quiets down when he hears their mother approach. And when Ferdie jumps up to be so helpful it's because he's trying to impress his mother; Martin firmly believes that he's only doing it to trick their mother into loving him more, and not because he's so much more the sterling type of character than Martin himself. The result is that Martin, thinking all these things, may very well allow his hatred for Ferdie to expand until it envelops his mother and even the idea of being helpful.

When you come right down to it, the jealous child constantly compares himself to the other children. He compares the amount of love he gets with the amount his brothers and sisters get. One may well take it for granted that he will firmly believe he isn't getting as much love and any parent who makes comparisons between him and the other children is only rubbing it in. Why bother to tell him that the others do things better than he does, when it's already so obvious to him that he is inadequate? After all, isn't it his very inadequacy which causes him to be loved less?

There are a number of expressions which I would like to see eliminated from the vocabulary of parents. As soon as they are aware that a second child is on the way they should practice forgetting how to say these things; five minutes a day, if they put their minds to it, would be fine.

Parents should forget all expressions ending in *than you*, such as *better than you, brighter than you, cleaner than you, more obedient than you, plays more nicely than you*, etc. Also, they should shun comparisons which begin with *not as* and end with *as you*, like *not as boisterous as you; not as noisy, willful, destructive*, etc., *as you*. And they should avoid the direct method of encouraging children to imitate their brothers; they should stop using expressions beginning with *See how*, like *See how he eats everything on his plate, See how he puts his things away*, etc.

Martin will one day tell his friends: "My brother Ferdie is bigger than anybody else's big brother, and he can lick anybody here." He has pride in his brother's superiority over other fellows' brothers; what we hope to achieve in the well-formed family is that he will have the same admiration for Ferdie's superiority over him. Unfortunately he may feel Ferdie is a threat to his security if he has heard too many times that Ferdie *is* better than he, because he assumes that Ferdie is loved more because he is better.

There may well be great differences in the athletic ability and intelligence of two children in the same family, but it won't matter, as long as the parents take pains *not* to point it out. When the less intelligent or less capable one is made aware that it is his own inadequacy which causes him to be less loved, he is in a very hopeless position. He can't win out, no matter how hard he tries. Sometimes he will resign from competition entirely, whereas another boy in the same position may decide to brazen it out, to capitalize on some questionable advantage or other, such as making up for lack of brains by development of muscular prowess. Such a boy may become strong and successful, too, but too often the hatred which forced him into this particular specialty makes him a bully.

To demonstrate how difficult it is to deal with the problem of avoiding comparisons, here is an example of a child fishing for a compliment.

"Don't you think Amy is pretty?" a little girl may ask, beaming at her baby sister. It's a trap. If one says, "Yes, she is," the child may say, "She's prettier than I am, isn't she?"

What the child wants is reassurance that she is prettier than Amy; she thinks that if she is prettier she will be loved more than Amy. Furthermore, she will try to do everything she can to win out in other comparisons between the two. The older child has an apparent advantage: she is usually old enough to think up tricks to make her appear to be a better child than her younger sister. Depending on the ages of the children, we usually find there is a tendency for the older child to imitate the baby, mostly by reverting to babyish habits, by using baby talk. In other words, she is inviting comparison and is saying, in effect, "Look at me; I'm more babyish than the baby, and I expect you to love me more."

Baby talk in a child who has been able to speak clearly and well is usually direct competition with the baby. Stuttering and stammering are also good indicators of a psychological disturbance in a child: tension of some sort is at the basis of the trouble, or it may be an unconscious expression of a desire to return to infancy. The child who is jealous, and therefore insecure, certainly wants to return to the infantile state where he was so very dependent and so very well cared for. Stuttering may be his imitation of the inarticulate speech of the infant. He is trying to say to his mother: "I'm weak and helpless and I need your love exclusively."

If you hear a child say: "My sister is beautiful. She has the nicest eyes, blond hair, and such a wonderful complexion," take a good look at her. You may find that she is herself very pretty, probably much prettier than her sister, and she is saying something which is completely untrue. Don't be misled; this isn't just a modest child, or an overly generous one. It is a child who has decided that her sister is more loved than she and can find no other explanation for it than the one she gives: her sister, she says, is better than she is. How does she come to this conclusion? She is, unfortunately, the victim of comparisons. She may have been told, as a disciplinary act when her mother was displeased with her behavior, that her sister was more this or a better that; her self-esteem is wounded because she may feel unable to compete with her sister. If she tries to be modest, or if she is too generous with her compliments to or about her sister, she may be looking for approval. But if she believes, really and truly, that her sister is all the things she says, it is a sign that she has given up the fight, that she is ready to neglect her beauty and the rest of it. She may become the withdrawn spinster sister who never marries and stays at home to be the "companion" of her aging parents.

Parents shouldn't be afraid to deny it when their child makes a statement like that; what's more important, they should get together with her to determine *why* she wants to think so. If she says she doesn't know why, or if she says she really believes it, they should talk to her about her jealousy, make her see that they know, and she should know, that she is jealous, that she is jealous because she thinks she is loved less than her sister. Above all, they should make sure that she knows she can feel more secure in the future. Parents do this by increasing the amount of attention they give her—they have to get across the idea to her that they *do* love her. It goes without saying that parents can't accomplish this unless they themselves know why they don't love her as much as they love the other child.

Parents must avoid comparisons and they must be quick to ferret out those inspired by the child himself. The oldest child in a group of three is "nicer" to the youngest one because being nicer gets him praise—but making the youngest his ally is also a good way of getting back at the middle child. In one family of two boys, for example, the father brought home a fine puppy one day. Georgie, who was seven, fell madly in love with him, and proceeded to work out his jealousy, too.

He did what he could to scare the daylights out of Tony, aged four, by telling him terrifying stories about dogs attacking little boys, with the result that Tony kept far, far away from the animal. He'd scream when Georgie brought the dog near him. Georgie now had an ally, too, against the younger brother, of whom he was jealous, but more than that he received his reward when his father would say, over and over again, "Georgie is braver than Tony." (Tony, by the way, has a choice of remaining timid for the rest of his life, or competing with Georgie to see who will be "braver.")

Comparisons can hardly be avoided when we are dealing with twins: we seem to want to do nothing but compare their similarities and their differences. When there is jealousy between the twins themselves it is most likely to be due to such comparisons.

When the jealousy of the other children in the family is

directed against the twins, the twins are looked upon as a single child, or as a unit, by the older brothers and sisters. This will happen especially when the twins are of the type known as "identical." Identical twins are developed from the same ovum; sometimes it's almost impossible to tell them apart. Fraternal twins are different: they develop from two different ova and they are usually no more alike than other brothers and sisters in the family, except for whatever similarities are the result of their being the same age. They can be of the same sex or of different sexes; identical twins are always the same sex.

All twins, like all children, come to demand that they be treated as individuals. It takes a little longer for identical twins to get around to it; actually they prefer to be treated as a unit, and attempts to treat them as individuals are so much wasted effort. This attitude is partly defensive, to protect themselves from the jealousy of the other children, but part of it is based on the advantage they have in being a center of attraction and cute, especially if they dress alike. When they begin to ask for suits or dresses which are not exactly alike it can be taken as a sign of their wish to grow apart. At some point or other in their growing up, identical twins become fed up with their cuteness and attracting attention; it is a very hopeful sign when they decide they no longer have to be cute. At that point their parents, if they are careful, will find that the twins are beginning to express differences in the kinds of friends they pick for each other, in their toys, their books, and their likes and dislikes.

When they are young, identical twins prefer not to be different from each other. The minutest difference between them is the more noticeable because they *are* so much alike. Sometimes parents try to search out, pounce upon, and emphasize a single distinguishing mark or blemish, just to be able to tell them apart, only to find that the twins have closed their ranks, so to speak: Robert broke his right upper front tooth this week, the same tooth that Roy broke three weeks ago, and now you can't tell them apart again.

Identical twins guard their similarities and preserve them. The more they look alike and act alike, the better their chances are that they will be loved alike. If both are mediocre, it is said to be due to the similarities in taste, temperament, intelligence, environment, and everything else. It may be, but it is also true that on any level one twin will not allow the other twin to be inferior to him for very long; if Robert wins the camp tennis championship, Roy is the runner-up; when Roy wins the backstroke, Robert is a close second. The reason is that twins are more acutely aware of how quickly they may become jealous of each other. They have to divide everything—love, understanding, protection, approval, security—perfectly equally between them, unlike other brothers and sisters, who get unequal amounts of these things because of the differences between them: differences in age, temperament, sex, appearance, and demands. Non-twin children (and nonidentical twins) emphasize how dissimilar they are from each other in order to gain some advantage over the others—more love, more security. Identical twins, as a unit, already have more love—at least they inspire more interest in themselves and therefore get more attention —and their only problem lies in the necessity of sharing it equally between them. Neither would like the other to be resentful, or jealous, because it would make them less similar. Their importance lies in their functioning as a unit; their existence as a unit depends on their remaining absolutely alike.

Naturally, they become self-centered, which is a phenomenon of identical twins just like a non-twin becoming self-centered. In twins it's twice as effective, there being twice as many selves; also, because of this, it's twice as easy for twins to feel left out of things, lonesome and apart from the rest of the world.

It is not only that they are bored with cuteness that makes them want to become individuals when they grow up, but also that there is no longer any advantage to remaining a unit. There are decided advantages from time to time; it is a protective measure when their brothers and sisters are jealous of them. Their need for mutual support becomes more impressive under such circumstances, so that there may be no recognizable difference between them until they are of high-school age, or even older. This is especially noticeable in families where there are a number of sets of twins: here the parents dress the twins alike even when they are quite grown up. Each pair of twins is treated as an individual unit by the other pairs of twins, and the rivalries and loves and hatreds between them are exactly the same as those in families where there are no twins. Some people who have been around such families get the impression that there is much more confusion and tension than in families without twins. The explanation is simple: you double the number of children and you double the amount of noise.

When nonidentical or fraternal twins are not permitted to be individuals, when they are treated as if they were identical twins, there may be jealousy between them. Such a case was the one in which the mother insisted that her dissimilar twins be treated like identical twins. She was an immature person and quite incapable of treating her children from an adult point of view. While she was pregnant her doctor told her that she would have twins. She was so delighted at the effect that they would create that she made plans far in advance of their birth to collect a lot of baby things intended to make them look as cute as possible.

She gave birth to two girls, but they were not identical twins. That didn't stop her. They were named Jane Ellen and Ellen Jane; she bought identical clothes for them and treated them for as long as she could as if they were identical twins. When the girls were four and a half months old, it was plain to see that Jane Ellen was the weaker and the more troublesome of the two. She was a feeding problem, couldn't gain weight, and was unable to sit up by the age of eight months. She didn't begin to walk until she was seventeen

months old; Ellen Jane got around very adequately at thirteen months and had begun to speak words plainly when she
was ten months old.

We can jump ahead to the time they were eight years old
and look at the report from the child-guidance clinic:

> The mother says that her children are a problem to her and
> she doesn't know what to do. Jane Ellen is noisy, disobedient,
> cries easily, can't get along with her teachers in school, and at
> the age of eight has suddenly started bed-wetting. The other
> children in the neighborhood refuse to play with her because
> she fights and bites them.

The case was easily handled because the doctor was able
to see very quickly that the mother was guilty of comparing
Jane Ellen to her healthier, stronger, and more appealing
sister. The only difference between this case and what happens to non-twins whose jealousy is intensified when they are
compared to each other is that Jane Ellen and Ellen Jane
were the same age. There were many dissimilar things about
them and rather than treat them as separate individuals their
mother tried to make them both alike.

Jane Ellen would tell her doctor that her sister was prettier
than she, which wasn't true, and that her sister had blond
hair, which wasn't true either.

"I'm coming here because I'm the dumb one in the family,
I guess," she told the doctor one day. "Everybody says so . . .
Mother, my teacher, everybody."

"You don't seem to be dumb to me," the doctor said.

"You don't know, that's all. I think of dumb things, too. I
wet my bed in my sleep once and that's how the whole thing
started."

"How do you mean?" he asked.

"Well, I was always so different from Ellen Jane from then
on. She *never* wet her bed—oh, no! Not until I taught her.
That's what makes Mommy so mad: I think of the worst
things to do and teach them to Ellen Jane."

So, not only did this child suffer from being compared to her sister, but also she was blamed for the bad things her sister did! It would follow, when you come to think of it: she is told that her sister is a paragon, that she is in every sense a perfect child, and that she would be perfect, too, if she were like her sister. When the paragon does bad things and Jane Ellen can't be compared to her, blame Jane Ellen for the badness.

These things were discussed with her mother, who one day made the following remarkable and intelligent speech, which proved that she understood her problem and would know how to deal with it:

"I always thought of what good I could get out of them," she told the doctor. "It's always what the neighbors will think, what my relatives will think; and that's why I have to make Jane Ellen behave better, like her sister. I've been thinking—'Suppose they weren't twins: would I still act the same way?' And I've decided I probably would. I've just been raising that twin business as an excuse to make things easier for me. If Jane Ellen was only three years old I'd still be saying, 'Why aren't you as neat as your big sister?' Well, just because these children were born at the same time doesn't mean they can't be two different people, with one of them good at some things, and the other one good at other things. . . . It would be easier for *me* if they were both alike, but I'm not making it easier for them."

When parents become aware of their children's problems usually half the battle is won; almost like magic they know what to do about them and why. Parents should put themselves in their children's place and imagine that they have come to them and said: "Look at the way Mrs. So-and-so treats her children. She *never* makes comparisons. Why can't you be kind and loving as she is?" Most parents would have to admit that this could make them resent Mrs. So-and-so. Then they should remember that children are even quicker to resent being compared to other children.

CHAPTER XVI

The "Average" Family

———◆———

IN THIS book I have tried to include most of the ways in which jealousy will show itself in children and I have tried to point out many of those things which can produce, or increase, jealousy and rivalry. Naturally, I couldn't hope to describe every possible situation, or to advise every family about all its problems. Each family is different from any other. Parents have different occupations, financial statuses, social lives, cultural backgrounds, and traditions, which will influence the way they live and think. These things must affect the way their children grow and develop, as well as the kinds of problems the children have to cope with.

Parents are worried today because they feel that most of what they were once taught about bringing up children is obsolete. They feel they have nothing to substitute for the ideas they have given up, or have begun to question. They try to be "good" parents and it seems an endless chore; they try being permissive and it doesn't work; in desperation they punish their children and feel guilty. With all the worries about places to live, bills to be paid, and food to be prepared, they have the additional burden of trying to devise a new set of rules for handling children. No wonder they feel that parenthood is a job which, at very best, is hard labor.

If parents can feel that children *will* flourish on attention and love, then they don't need to scold them constantly, or plead, or punish them, and parenthood becomes a very enjoyable venture. One does need to know how children develop and what to expect or not to expect at various age levels; it *does* take more time to reassure a child than to slap him for a misdeed. But it is far easier on one's own life: spending time with children doesn't have to produce an emotionally exhausted or unhappy parent. Anger, anxiety, oversolicitude, constant ordering, and constant forbidding are the chores which make family life a trial and a burden.

Loving their children doesn't mean that parents have to cushion them from the ups and downs of everyday human relationships. Children have to learn that unhappiness can rear its ugly head from time to time. But they shouldn't feel embittered and hopeless about it. The best models for children are their parents, who not only teach them the basic aspects of living, but also how to live happily. Obviously children shouldn't have to use as a model parents who don't know how to get along with each other. Children can therefore be expected to have difficulties as a result of their parents' troubles in dealing with each other. But when parental disagreements are open, frank, and honest expressions of annoyance, a child can learn a good deal, provided that he is convinced—and provided his parents are convinced—that there is deep affection between them and that the strife is only temporary. In fact, such acting out of feelings is infinitely more helpful to parents and children than making believe with sweetness and light. The child who sees nothing but sweetness and light can get the impression that his sudden and temporary hatred of his brothers and sisters is abnormal and that he will always be a bad boy. Children should be taught that hatred and anger, openly expressed, can be temporary things and not at all sinful.

It should always be borne in mind that what we want in the relationship between children is friendship between them and friendship doesn't necessarily mean that they will have to love each other in spite of everything. They will be quicker to develop a friendly feeling toward each other if they are not convinced, from the attitudes of their parents and relatives, that they are wicked because they occasionally hate. It is for this reason that parents must rid themselves of the idea that their children should be forced to love each other no matter what. Also, children will get an idea of what friendship is like if their parents are honest in their feelings toward each other. When the wife can express her opinion of her husband's thoughtlessness about failing to call up when he was late for dinner, or staying out too late at his club, and when the husband can rant a bit about the bills his wife is running up, their children will be impressed. Their parents can get angry and, in the children's eyes, "hate" each other, but a few days or hours or even minutes later they are the same loving and understanding people they always were. If such behavior, including "hate," is permitted in parents, it can be a very valuable and graphic lesson for their children.

The role of parents is essentially this: they must represent orderly living and embody the kind of loving authority that makes for free people and mature adults. They have to respect and develop the child's capacities for being good, kind, and generous—capacities which *every* child possesses. They must be happy with each other. They must not let their own emotional disturbances blind them to the needs of their children who are dependent upon them, and they must not rationalize unfairness and unkindness or punishment as being good for the child.

In almost every case history of jealousy in children which has become a problem, it is a reflection of the parents' problems and not primarily the child's. Scratch a problem child and you may find a problem parent. One of my professors in medical school used to repeat, over and over again, when discussing diseases of children, "If a child does this or that, or thus and so, start treating the parents." He would start off a lecture on temper tantrums of children by saying, "When a child has too many temper tantrums, start treating his parents." To quote this professor further: "Unfortunately, it's very difficult to get parents to understand. I told one young father, whose son was five and still a bed wetter, that I felt that he and his wife should be treated. 'Look here,' said the young man, 'I brought my son here for a physical checkup. There's nothing wrong with bed wetting; it's hereditary in my family. Why, I used to wet my bed until I was eight.' Well, all I can say now is what I thought of then: that the problems of his parents were visited on him, just as his problems were being visited on his child. It isn't hereditary, but it's extremely contagious!"

Besides the great difficulty in making parents see where they are to blame, there is the added factor of relatives, friends, and servants. Sometimes the situation becomes rather exasperating when parents find their efforts to do everything right are nullified by some outsider who has no conception of what has been going on. For example, let me present the story of the Jenkins family. The young parents had made every effort to find the best way to handle the arrival of their second child, only to be thwarted not only by their in-laws but also by the nurse. Emily was two years old, a happy child, well loved, protected, and apparently with few problems. Her parents were naturally anxious to preserve her happiness as much as possible and to minimize the shock that the arrival of the baby would most certainly bring on. Of course, she was too young to understand all the sexual and physical details of the birth process, but she knew enough to be mildly impressed with the fact that Mommy had a baby inside her. She looked forward to the baby's arrival with curiosity. There was no reason to feel that the baby was going to be a threat to her.

While the mother was away at the hospital having the baby, two things happened which upset all the preparations. First of all, both grandmothers were in competition with each other for Emily's and the new baby's favors: they began to bring presents to the house for Emily, announcing that they were from her baby brother. Apparently this was intended to make Emily like her new baby brother, by impressing her with his generosity. In other words, it was a series of bribes: the implication was that if she didn't like the baby brother after he arrived home, she was nothing but an ungrateful little so-and-so, after he had been so nice as to go out and buy a lot of toys especially for her. Whoever thought up this plan didn't realize how silly it was: Emily had a pre-formed picture of anyone who gave her gifts, and this was going to conflict with reality. Instead of a baby, smaller than she and much more helpless, she would expect to find a grown person, like the other grown people who brought her presents. It would be only natural for her to dismiss from her mind any inkling that the newly arrived infant had anything to do with the gifts she got, supposedly from him, but obviously—to her—from someone else named "New Baby," that mysterious benefactor who was a cross between Dad and Uncle John.

If the grandmothers had let it go at that, everything would have been fine, and no great harm would have been done, but again their own problems made it impossible for them to accept defeat gracefully: to them it was defeat when Emily showed signs of being jealous of Tommy, the new baby. It was some time before Mr. and Mrs. Jenkins discovered what had been happening. Remember, these parents were well aware that Emily was going to be jealous of her brother; they were willing to accept her jealousy for what it was worth and to deal with it when it arose, with as little damage to Emily's self-esteem as possible. Then one day Mr. Jenkins' mother arrived at the house and went through the following conversation, almost word for word like a subsequent conversation between his mother-in-law and Emily a day later:

"Emily, don't you love your cute baby brother, Tommy?" her grandmother asked.

"No, I don't," said Emily. "I sat on him and he cried and I did bad and he cried."

"Why, Emily! After all those nice presents he brought you!"

Emily's father shifted uneasily in his seat. "Mother," he said, "what do you hear from Aunt Martha? Is she coming here for the holidays?"

His mother was still shocked by Emily's ingratitude; she

said, "Aunt Martha—Aunt Martha? Oh, yes, Aunt Martha. I haven't heard yet. Don't you think Emily is a bad little girl because she doesn't love her little brother?"

"No, I don't," her son told her, looking straight at Emily while he spoke. "Emily doesn't have to like him."

Then he took his mother gently by the arm and led her into the kitchen; she had a "Well, I never!" look on her face. He began to explain that Emily had a right not to like her brother, that she was jealous of him, and that it was perfectly all right. He tried to explain to her that Emily's jealousy was a problem that both he and his wife would handle and that she didn't have to bother with it.

The poor boy was up against tremendous odds. It was very hard to convince his mother that she didn't know best, that Emily was not a little problem child because she didn't like her brother. But he persisted and he won a small victory. His mother promised that she would let Emily hate Tommy, provided the rival grandmother was given the same instructions. Some grandparents hate to have their authority challenged. Some of them appear to feel responsible for their children's actions, but only where it shows. It's more a question of how it will look to the neighbors, what friends will think, or "I brought him up better than that." This is exactly where much of the problem of grandparents comes in: it's the attempt to cover up an unconscious feeling of guilt that they weren't satisfactory parents, that they may have made mistakes in bringing up their own children. They cover it up— or try to, anyway—by registering a good deal of disapproval of the superficial and outward behavior of their children, especially after they get married. When his mother-in-law arrived, poor Jenkins had to go through almost exactly the same thing, following an almost identical conversation between her and Emily, but this time he had to appeal to his wife to help him explain things.

But this wasn't all. It was some time later that they discovered the sabotage that had been inspired by Nurse and which started some time before Tommy came home from the hospital. In order to get Emily to behave, Nurse began calling attention to the arrival of someone better than Emily, better behaved, better mannered, and more obedient. She would say to her, "I'll bet the baby won't make any fuss about drinking his milk. . . . When he gets here I won't like you so much, because you're a bad girl. . . . It will be a relief to see somebody nice around this house for a change." And then, to corroborate Emily's apprehension about her brother after he came home, the Nurse told her, "He's much nicer than you are, and not half as much trouble. . . . Everybody likes him better than they like you because you make such a fuss about things. . . . I'm sure he wouldn't act that way if he were your age."

Here was another example of an adult pushing her own problems onto a child. Her problems? It was more than just her refusal to recognize her shortcomings as a nurse. She had to resort to the device of pitting Emily against her brother, creating a problem between them, in order to get Emily to obey what were, after all, rather unimportant and trivial commands; most likely they were not necessary to Emily's well-being. But the nurse was one of those people who cannot bear to see their authority undermined, especially by a child. When she gave a command, she intended that it be obeyed; parents who have this need to see all of their instructions carried out, promptly, without question, sometimes resort to beating their children when they are disobedient.

Beatings are no worse than what the nurse did when she compared Emily and her infant brother; it's sometimes just as bad to compare the behavior, the obedience, or the complete subjugation, of the one child with the other. It isn't so much a question of getting a child to obey your orders as it is: Do your orders *have* to be obeyed?

This need to feel important leads to many difficulties, the greatest of which is inconsistency. "The need to feel important" is most usually the result of one's own insecurity and feelings of low self-esteem. Apparently some individuals think they can salvage their self-respect by giving the appearance of being important to those around them, by trying to impress others by fakery; some respond to this urge by becoming boastful, some by lying about their exploits, and some by demanding authority in their contacts at home, at work, and with their friends. Like other neurotic drives, it's an insatiable need, because the victim has to be given signs of his importance over and over and over again. He probably is not satisfied to have just one of his commands obeyed, because, unconsciously, he thinks that it may be an accident. "After all," says the unconscious, "who am I, really, that this person has to obey me? Let me try again." And so the demand is made in all directions, with all contacts.

Children suffer most when they have parents who are afflicted this way. The need for authority sneaks up on the sufferer when he least expects it, without warning and at a moment's notice. That's why such people are inconsistent in their dealings with children. For example, there are times when a parent may laugh approvingly at something his child does: his son has just learned a new song at school and has sung it at home for the first time. He is glad that his parents are proud of him, and on Sunday, when his father is reading the newspaper, he sings the song over and over because he wants to get approval again. He is told three times to stop; he can't understand why he is told to stop singing, when this is the very thing he did a few days ago that brought him applause and approval. Perhaps, he thinks to himself, they didn't hear him correctly, so he'll do it again. Or, he may think, if he is at all reasonable, that these are very mixed-up people who don't know how to make up their minds: first it's one thing, then it's another; he'll sing it in spite of them. No matter what goes on in the child's mind, what happens to the father is disastrous to the child: the father's commands are disobeyed, willfully, and for no reason that he can think of. All the father knows is that he is being thwarted, that his authority is questioned, that he is being disobeyed, and is therefore losing some of his sought-after importance. So the child gets a spanking.

Inconsistency must be avoided at all costs. In homes where parents are inconsistent in their dealings with their children, jealousy becomes a very serious problem: here, more than anywhere else, the parent is more likely to blame one child for something that the other child has done. Somewhere along the line children get the idea that they have done things they shouldn't have done and they feel that these things merit punishment. The fact that some of these real or imaginary villainies have been overlooked by their parents doesn't remove their guilt feelings completely; sometimes their misdeeds are purposely overlooked by their parents, who may not feel in the mood to punish the child at that particular moment. When a child has amassed enough guilty feelings about enough wrongdoing, he has, at the same time, convinced himself that he is a bad boy because he is so capable of doing evil things. As I pointed out before, and as others have pointed out before me, children need to be prevented from doing bad things and they appreciate the help of anyone who keeps them from being bad. At the same time, children will build up many excuses and defenses for their wickedness, in the event that they are ever called upon to explain themselves. For a parent to make a mistake and punish a child for something he hasn't done, at just such a time, is catastrophic. The child musters all of his well-hoarded defenses of the things he really did that *were* bad, and for which he was not punished, and is righteously indignant for being punished for something he didn't do. At the same time he feels martyred along with feeling hatred for his parents, who punished him unjustly.

Some of the statistical studies on the occurrence of jealousy show that consistency in disciplining children is most important; it doesn't matter, apparently, what form of discipline is used. Inconsistency in disciplining children is one of the most common causes of jealousy. Of all the methods of discipline, the most dangerous is to compare children with each other. But even comparisons don't emphasize the problem of jealousy as much as using any form of discipline without a definite and consistent plan. In other ways, children suffer more from their parents' changing their horsewhips, as it were, in midstream. When they disregard, or even approve of, the child's behavior at one time, they must never punish the child for doing the same thing some other time.

Statistics also show that jealousy is most serious in a family where the parents play favorites. Sometimes a parent makes the child who most resembles him the favorite child. This can be another problem of a problem parent: it is closely related to a daydream that some people indulge in, a daydream of having a twin. The person who likes to have this kind of daydream is highly flattered by his resemblance to other people, and would be especially fond of a child who resembled him. In our psychoanalytic work we have found that such people are lonely people, and that their desire for a twin (or their preference for the child who resembles them) is based on a childhood desire for companionship, when there wasn't enough companionship, or love, in childhood. So the parent who favors one child over the others may be doing it because it happens to be a problem of his which has never been worked out, and which affects his relationships not only with his children but with other adults.

Each child differs from the other children in the family because of the events surrounding each child's birth, his attitude toward his parents, his attitude toward each succeeding child, and the attitude of each of those children toward the ones who came before. It is important that parents recognize that these differences exist; rather than play favorites they should isolate the problem children from the others and make some effort to help those children who need it.

This means work, harder work than parents are accustomed to do on behalf of their children, in too many cases. It is, after all, much easier to pay more attention to the child who doesn't have problems, who is able to get along, and who isn't a constant reminder that something has gone wrong in the parents' treatment of their children. The unfortunate victim is the one who needs help most, and this help may have to be given him subtly, without calling too much attention to it, so that the other children aren't adversely affected. He should receive special favors wherever possible, not because he has to be appeased, but because he deserves special favors. Parents should realize that it is most likely something they have forgotten to do that has caused him to be this way and it is only right that they correct the mistakes they have made. Children are quick to suspect appeasement, and one shouldn't try to fool them.

More than anything else, parents have to convince their relatives and friends that no child is to be made a favorite child, no matter what problems the relatives or friends may have. Too many times relatives tend to line up on the side of the child, again, who resembles their branch of the family. The best thing to do is to warn these people, or cajole them, or threaten them, and eventually, if necessary, lock them out of the house. They should not be allowed back in until the children can cope with the problems of the adults around them, which is when the children are adults themselves.

Mostly, jealous children think that they have been rejected by their parents, or feel that they are not the favorite child—or both. It's hard to separate these two things, especially because they are frequently found to be present together: make one child the favorite and the child who isn't the favorite feels rejected. Sometimes a parent who has had an unhappy childhood can be unconsciously resentful of his children's attempts at happiness, or he may be resentful that one child behaves the way he did as a child, proving him to be a bad parent himself. His resentment may make him take it out on the child. Parents whose freedom has been curtailed when the babies arrive and who resent these new responsibilities are too frequently immature people who have never been able to accept *any* responsibilities; such parents will reject their children, too. As I mentioned before, the largest group of children that feel rejected is those who were unwanted babies.

Some of the problems of mothers who reject their children

arise from such things as resentment of marriage and motherhood because it has completely destroyed any chance for a
professional career. Or the mother who has married a social
inferior, or someone higher in the social plane than herself,
may look upon the child either as an upstart or as a snob.
And then there are also the mothers who are sexually incom-
patible with their husbands, who look upon sex itself with
distaste and look upon their children as perpetual reminders
of a series of unpleasant incidents. There are whole lists of
such problems—some of them problems of the mother and
some of them problems of the father, many of them problems of both mothers and fathers—but the important thing
to remember is this: the child who is made to feel inferior
by his parents for any reason, whether it be *unconscious* rejection of him by the parents or a bald statement from them
that he is not as good as the favored brother or sister, is the
child who will suffer most from jealousy.

One of the most difficult problems that parents have to deal
with in themselves can best be described as an attempt to
make their children grow up in accordance with the ideas
that the parents have had, rather than to accept the fact that
the children are individuals. They would like to have their
children turn out to be quiet and obedient, or gay and viva-
cious; studious, or athletic—or something equally flattering
to the parents themselves. They may be shocked that their
daughter reaches the age of seven and is a high-spirited,
boisterous, quite unladylike creature, resembling none of
the females on either side of the family. And sometimes it is
such a disappointment for a father who has looked forward
to having a son who will relish going to the north woods with
him when he grows up, fishing, and camping, and living out
in the open, when the boy prefers books and at the age of
thirteen can discuss jet propulsion at the dinner table.

The disappointment and frustration that parents feel is
the result, again, of their need to be important. They have
a wish to have a child who resembles them in nature, personality, and character, if not in appearance, as if to confirm

their opinion that their own way of life is good, so good that it has been adopted as a way of life by their children. That's why they feel hurt that the child should find some way of life other than that suggested by his parents: it's obviously a reflection on his parents' good judgment. In a family where there are a number of children, one of them at least is going to get the idea that he can get more favors by following his parents' wishes. He's right, too, and the result is that the other children may feel rejected and are jealous.

Children do reach a point where they begin to recognize that their parents are playing fair and square with them, even though they may give one child more advantages than the other. Such children must have confidence in their parents' ability to deal justly with them. Forcing one's children to play with each other, to take care of each other, and to have the same friends, leaves them without any status as individuals. Parents who have a crying need within themselves to force their children to conform to a pattern are doing so because of unsolved conflicts which they are taking out on their children; they are going to be as unsuccessful as those dictators who attempt to destroy individuality and create a world of formless, soulless, automatic beings who are somewhat less than human.

There are so many practical aspects that have to be considered. By making sure the children know that they are different from each other parents can avoid many very serious problems. For example, the younger children may feel rejected when the older ones are given more sophisticated toys, or are allowed to stay up later, or go on trips. Or girls in a family may resent being kept at girlish pursuits while their brothers are allowed more freedom. One child may grow up to crave a little less home life and a little less dependency on his parents, so that it may be necessary to send him to a boarding school. How can this be done without arousing great feelings of jealousy and cries of "Favoritism!" from the other children, who will be much better off in public school? The answer is that children who know that their parents are dealing fairly with them, children who have confidence in their parents' love for them, will be able to see and even appreciate the fact that their parents are respecting the needs of each one as an individual.

This is another of those things which require a good deal of patience and understanding, because it means convincing the children that there are differences between them. It isn't easy. A baby doesn't know and doesn't care that he is younger than the other children. As he grows older he will want their toys and later he will want their privileges. He must be told, therefore, over and over again: "You will have toys like these [or books, or more freedom] when you grow up." Actually, it works both ways: the older child has to be told that he has to put his own things away, despite the fact that his mother puts the younger one's things away for him. "I do it for him because he's still too young," the mother should tell the older one. "When you were his age I put your things away and when he's a few years older he'll put his own things away."

So with the girl in the family who resents her brothers' greater freedom, or the boy who thinks his sisters are being coddled while he is imposed on to do various unpleasant tasks. It takes time, but it's important that the children learn that there are certain things boys are permitted to do and other things girls are permitted to do. "I don't love you less because you're a boy," one mother told her son. "Girls need more dresses than boys need suits. Boys are stronger, too. You can carry heavier packages from the grocery store while she helps me with some of the housework."

This doesn't mean, of course, that children have to be made to accept these differences without a struggle on their part. Naturally they will resent whatever advantages the other children have, for a time. It requires patience: they must be reminded over and over again that there *are* differences. It requires understanding: they should be shown that there are certain benefits they derive from being older, being younger, being a boy, or being a girl.

Grandparents and other relatives are among the worst offenders in the matter of favoritism, and too often they can undo any or all of the good work done by the parents. Both sides of the family want to have the grandchild on their side, so to speak, and will use all sorts of cajolery and flattery to win over the child. Or, as sometimes happens, they will divide up the children between them, so that a problem is created which will make for even more jealousy. If they are made grandparents before they reach the age of fifty they have special problems of their own and, whether they know it or not, they usually take it out on the first grandchild. Reaching grandparenthood makes some of them worry: it is the sign of aging which impresses them more than any other. All of us can laugh off being called middle-aged when we are in our late thirties, and most of us are quite grateful that forty has been given so much favorable publicity: we grasp at the hope that *here* is where life begins, as the book said.

Even when our children are grown, we are not impressed too much with the approach of senility; we tend to narrow the distance between our age and theirs until we are all of the same generation. Incidentally, we rarely permit them to join us in our generation: it flatters us to condescend to theirs, sometimes to the embarrassment and the discomfort of our children. We shouldn't flatter ourselves that we are an exclusive group because we have more years. I've said it before: emotional maturity is not a matter of age alone and when parents welcome a son or a daughter to their generation it means that the children have to be accepted as mature people. It means that they are now as mature as their parents and not—as they are so often embarrassed into believing—that the parents are cultivating immaturity to descend to their level.

The worst offenders are grandmothers who are left to bring up a grandchild, or mothers who are almost forty when a daughter is born. The mother who is in her twenties when her daughter is born is more apt to welcome her daughter as her contemporary when the daughter reaches the age of fifteen, while the mother is still in her thirties. They are contemporaries; physiologically they are the same age, because they are both now capable of bearing children. Without being completely conscious of it, a young mother who is still able to bear children will unconsciously look upon her daughter who is reaching physical maturity as an equal more or less: both are capable of similar experiences. The young mother is virtually forced to accept her daughter as her equal, even though, superficially, she may hate her daughter's growing up, on the grounds that she "looks too young to be the mother of a grown daughter." However, by so doing she admits she has a rival—who is her equal.

This isn't true when there is a grandmother who has the sole charge of a granddaughter, or when the mother is in her forties. Such women are past the childbearing age when the young girl grows into it; they are intolerant of her potentialities, because childbearing is now a thing of the past for them. They look on it regretfully, or as a stage that one goes through when young. So, as far as they are concerned, the girl grows up to be a mother but is still referred to as "the baby." It is surprising to see how many immature women are the result of being brought up by much older people.

So many times common sense has been praised for the great good it does and can do in the bringing up of children, but it isn't always enough. A friend of mine, who was brought up on common sense and little real understanding, felt that he needed help but didn't want to be psychoanalyzed. I saw him some time later, after he had been to a psychiatrist, and asked him what had changed his mind.

It happened after his second child was born. His wife was much more interested in the problems of bringing up children than he was and went for advice to a child-guidance clinic near where they lived. After talking to one of the workers there, she made very careful preparation, so that their son would know that a baby was arriving. Her husband told me that he thought this was a lot of foolishness at the time, but he also told me that he had been convinced that it worked, especially in her treatment of the boy after the baby was born. He co-operated with her when she requested it, and they never showed any affection for the baby when their son was around.

"It must have had some effect on our son," my friend told me. "He believed us when we told him we loved him, and he believed us when we told him that he could be jealous of the baby. He could see that, and he realized, I suppose, that the baby was one of those necessary evils."

When the baby was about four months old, the parents took themselves and the two children to visit my friend's own parents out West. While they were there, my friend was amazed to hear his mother compliment them on the way their son was so obviously fond of the baby.

"It isn't as if the child went out of his way to take care of her, or to fondle her, or anything like that," my friend said. "You could see that he liked her. He would sit and watch her, and he'd beam at her, and he'd always call us if he thought that she needed some attention. Also, you could see that the baby liked him. She always smiled at him, and that flattered him. I never realized that two kids in a family could be that fond of each other, even at that age, although it's one of those things you hope for."

Evidently he was no less impressed by the phenomenon than his mother was, because after a few days she turned to him and his wife and said, "My, what a difference between your son and you. You probably don't remember, but when your baby brother was born you hated him so much that we had to do everything we possibly could to keep you out of his room. You were *such* a bad boy, you were so jealous."

This impressed my friend. In the first place, he realized that his wife's preparations were good, even if they were based on what some people referred to as newfangled psychological ideas. In the second place, and what was more important, he knew that he had violently hated his younger brother; he began to realize that some of the things that bothered him might have been the result of his common-sense upbringing. What had worked so well for his own child could very well be helpful to him, and he decided to go to a psychiatrist for help with his personal problems. Common sense is no substitute for understanding, especially where common sense means prejudice, custom, and rote, as well as a refusal to admit that one may be wrong. This is true in jealousy in children as well as in every other phase of living.

For parents, a final word: we know today that children can become worth while, well adjusted, and emotionally mature human beings, or destructive, antisocial, and unhappy ones, depending on what is done to them in their childhood. Competitiveness and aggression may be caused by childhood jealousy and rivalry; they may result in a search for power which can never be satisfied. This places a grave responsibility on parenthood. If parents guide their children toward ideals of fairness and equality, they will be contributing to the happiness of future generations and helping to bring about the peace and freedom which are the goals of the civilized world.

Index